# Grandpa Ganja's High School Survival Guide

by

Evan Keliher

Pedagogue Press P.O. Box 28808 San Diego, CA 92198

Copyright 2006 Evan Keliher

Cover Design by Steve Lopez, Hemet, CA

All rights reserved, no part of this book may be reproduced or transmitted in any form or by any means, electronic or mechanical, including photocopying, recording, or by any information storage and retrieval system without written permission from the author, except for the inclusion of brief quotations in a review.

ISBN: 978-0-9648859-2-9

SAN: 298-8054

Library of Congress Catalog
Card Number: 2006904275

Printed in the United States of America

Other works by Evan Keliher

**Books**
Grandpa's Marijuana Handbook
Guerrilla Warfare for Teachers
The De-Balling of America

**Feature Film**
*Rebel High*
Montreal, Canada

**Video**
*Grandpa's Marijuana Handbook (the movie)*
San Diego, California

**Plays**
*Witte's End*
*Sandwiched Light*

See additional online sitcoms/plays/screenplays
www.grandpaspotbook.com

# Table of Contents

| Chapter | Page |
|---|---|
| Introduction | 6 |
| 1. The Teachers | 8 |
| 2. Exams | 12 |
| 3. Grades | 17 |
| 4. Cheating | 23 |
| 5. Counselors | 32 |
| 6. Teachers, Wanton | 38 |
| 7. Classroom Seating | 41 |
| 8. Clubs | 45 |
| 9. Gym | 52 |
| 10. Truancy | 58 |
| 11. Holdups | 65 |
| 12. Johns | 68 |
| 13. Summer School | 72 |
| 14. Sex Education | 74 |
| 15. Homework | 80 |
| 16. The Curriculum - An Overview | 87 |
| 17. Weapons in Schools | 99 |
| 18. Substitute Teachers | 104 |
| 19. Prayer in School | 108 |
| 20. Principals | 111 |
| 21. Class Conduct | 115 |
| 22. Hall Passes | 121 |
| 23. Dating | 125 |
| 24. Parent Conferences | 126 |

| Chapter | | Page |
|---|---|---|
| 25. | Fire Drills | 129 |
| 26. | Lying | 134 |
| 27. | Parking | 138 |
| 28. | Extortionists/Bullies | 140 |
| 29. | Class Schedules | 145 |
| 30. | In-School Sales - Be An Entrepreneur | 149 |
| 31. | The Cafeteria | 152 |
| 32. | Apple Polishers | 155 |
| 33. | Drugs | 158 |
| 34. | Hall Lockers | 166 |
| 35. | Senior Trips | 168 |
| 36. | The Prom | 171 |
| 37. | After Graduation What? | 175 |
| | Epilogue | 177 |

## Introduction

As we all know, there are thousands of books out there telling you how to fix your own plumbing, get ahead in business, buy a used car, get laid, grow better house plants, and so on. These books are very useful, especially if you happen to have bad plumbing, need a promotion, are looking for a good used car, suffer from unrequited love, or have a lot of dead house plants on your hands.

Useful as they are, though, most of them are written for older people who have jobs, plumbing and houses. What value are these books to the average high school student in America?

It's clear that what's needed is a book aimed at those of you who are still teenagers struggling with what everybody acknowledges is the most trying and difficult time in a person's life, i.e., the four (or more!) years a kid spends in an American high school.

You guys need a book that deals with the reality of being a teenager in high school today, one that pulls no punches and tells the truth as it really is. Well, Grandpa Ganja is your man. It happens that there is no more qualified person in the country to write such a book than this author, as I taught kids just like you for thirty years in Detroit where education is at its most challenging.

While I've seen school at its worst and dealt with every form of madness imaginable, I must admit that I've had little experience with so-called good schools where real students attend classes regularly and do their homework religiously and have unblemished complexions.

Accordingly, this book is necessarily written from a point of view provided by working with armed and dangerous students, befuddled teachers, half-witted and usually incompetent administrators, unstable parents, and a central board of education inhabited entirely by lunatics and fatuous dopes.

The opinions are Grandpa Ganja's alone, the advice practical, the incidents real. If you're in high school now or are planning to go to high school anytime soon, this book is for you. It's chock full of schemes and plots and original ideas that will help you resist the assholes who are out to get you, the ones giving you all those Fs and writing snide notes about you to your parents and marking you absent just because you weren't there.

Outrageous, and you won't stand for it, by God!

## Chapter One

### THE TEACHERS

It helps to know the enemy. Forewarned is forearmed, as they say. Find out what makes them tick, how they think, where they're coming from, and you'll have that crucial edge needed to survive in the harsh world of high school.

Okay, where do teachers come from? They come from the middle class, that's where, and they're dripping with middle-class values. Teachers are against almost everything you think is fun, mostly because it's a lot of stuff they're no longer interested in themselves or because it's stuff they can no longer do.

They're against beer drinking, cutting classes, dope smoking, getting laid, loitering, original hairstyles, slang, loud music, and all those things that take the dreariness out of life and make the whole business more tolerable. And they're determined that you won't do any of these things, either, at least not if they have anything to say about it.

The real problem is, of course, that most teachers are old-timers, people of another generation who never do see eye to eye with teenagers. This is especially true nowadays since most of the younger teachers were fired in the last several years when enrollments declined as they did. Only old duffers kept their jobs and old people tend to be conservative and cynical because they've seen the world as it really is while young people are hopeful and optimistic because they haven't. As long as you have this generation gap, you'll have trouble between them.

Anyway, nature has decreed the rivalry and you're stuck with it. Your only chance is to outsmart them, and to do that you'll need to use your head for something besides a hat rack—a feat not easily accomplished by most people.

We'll begin by taking a closer look at the aforementioned old-timers, a group conveniently divided into (a) senile old bats and (b) sharp, eagle-eyed old pros who ask no quarter and give none. It's easy to tell them apart: one is sane and we're not sure about the other.

The senile old bats include teachers of assorted races, creeds, and sexes, and are not restricted to female old bats even though they outnumber the men because there are more women teachers generally. Most of them have been teaching for decades. Some of them were half-mad from the start while others were driven mad by the system—the very same system that's driving you mad, I might add.

If you're looking for the easy way out, sign up for the classes taught by the senile old bats. You won't have to do any work in their classes because they'll never ask you to. They spend twenty minutes taking attendance and trying to establish some order (something they never succeed in doing) and the rest of the period mucking about with some formless lesson designed to kill the remaining time.

As senile old bats are delighted when you do any work at all, it's easy to hand in a few copied assignments and a used book report and end up with an A or B.

You won't learn a thing in these classes, of course, but you won't do anything, either. A lot of jocks and bikers show up with the senile old bats, and all of the thugs and hooky players, too. The only problem you'll have is trying to get a seat in these classes, as they tend to fill up early.

A further consideration, of course, is that you'll spend the entire semester surrounded by some of the lowest IQs in Christendom and suffer nausea trying to breathe air polluted by the presence of bikers, a group widely known for being unfamiliar with soap.

The second group of old-timers, the sharp, eagle-eyed old pros, are a different story altogether. These old bats have been around as long as their senile colleagues, but the resemblance ends there. These dudes are old-timers who've kept their wits about them and actually gotten sharper over the years. Everybody in school knows who they are; their reputations precede them.

Naturally, everybody wants to avoid their classes if at all possible because these teachers will fail your ass and everybody knows it. Many a kid has suffered the humiliation of being ordered off the stage at graduation time when one of these guys showed up with the last minute results of his final exam.

The old pros were good teachers when they were younger and they still are. They're tough disciplinarians, they don't put up with any crap. If you wrong them they'll pursue you to the ends of the Earth to see justice done. They run their classes with an iron fist and scowl a lot. They demand that you work like hell and they'll flunk you every time if you don't.

If you're actually interested in learning something, these are the teachers to take. And don't worry, there's always plenty of room in their classes.

## Chapter Two

### Exams

Now that you've had a brief opening glimpse of the people who run the place and have the most to do with your overall ruin, you need to direct your attention to a matter that will cause you more trouble than any other in your high school career: exams and the attendant grades that accompany them. There are only a few kinds of basic formal examinations found in the average high school, and you need to take a close look at all of them.

The first of these is the classic essay exam. This one is good for people that know how to write because that's what is required on this kind of test. You're given a question to answer on some general topic and you have to fill up three or four pages in answering it.

You don't actually have to know the answer, of course, and that's the beauty of this kind of test. All you have to do is come up with enough bullshit that's even loosely connected with the subject under discussion and you pass. Use jargon where possible.

If it's a history exam use terms related to this field such as circa, sixteenth-century, white man's burden, imperialism, and so on. Make up fictional sources and quote them; if your teacher's like most she's not likely to go to the trouble of checking them out.

One ruse that works like a charm is to use barely legible handwriting, a device easy for most of you since the average high school student today already has handwriting that defies deciphering. There's nothing teachers hate more than struggling to figure out what the hell the kid has written. In fact, most teachers would rather give you the benefit of the doubt than go blind trying to analyze your writing and this bit of knowledge can save your ass if you play it right.

For instance, suppose you're given one of those fill in the blank tests where a word is missing and you're required to supply it. Let's say the question is, "The first message sent by the newly invented telegraph was, 'What hath God _____?'"

Okay, suppose you remember it started with a w or an r but you can't come up with the exact word. All you do is write something like *wroshern* or *rowrusa* or even *wassefnr* in letters that closely resemble Egyptian hieroglyphics and the teacher will give up and mark it right out of sheer desperation.

But what if she decides to mark it wrong anyway? In that case, you immediately take your paper up for a rehearing and demand that you wrote *wrought* and you want credit, by God. If you're firm enough and refuse to back down, the beleaguered teacher will invariably give in and mark it right just to get you to shut the hell up and give her some peace.

Essay exams have some good points but only if you can write. If you can't write, or if you write no better than about 80% of the population as a whole, you're better off looking for teachers who are known to give so-called objective-type exams such as the above mentioned fill in the blank tests, the kind that don't require you to write more than two or three words at a time.

The true-false test is the ultimate objective exam. Teachers love this kind of test because it's so easy to correct. They just slap a key on the damn thing and count up all the correct answers. (Some teachers prefer to count all the errors but that always takes longer—at least it does at Cody where I taught.) These exams will surely continue to be popular as long as a lot of your teachers are lazy, i.e., forever.

True-false exams are guessing games. Even the school half-wit can get 50% right if he can just smuggle a coin into the exam. Heads it's A, tails B. The law of averages works in your favor. And if you've done any studying at all you're bound to know a few of the answers going in, an advantage which, coupled with the 50% figure, will enable you to pass any given true-false test.

Another objective test is the multiple-choice one, an exam offering four or more choices on each question. These tests are somewhat harder than true-false ones and require more thought. For one thing, pure guessing will get you a score of 25% and that's not a passing score even at Cody where we usually passed everyone with good attendance. It's clear that you need to do more than merely guess on a multiple-choice test.

Well, you can. Most multiple-choice tests have at least one answer in the four provided that's obviously wrong. Consider this question on an American history test.

Q. The man known as The Father of Our Country was

    a. Thomas Edison    b. Benjamin Franklin
    c. Oliver Cromwell    d. George Washington

Okay. Let's assume you don't know the answer—in most cases a safe assumption—but you do recognize at least three of those names. Since it's pretty likely you would recognize the name of the Father of our Country if you saw it and you don't recognize this Cromwell dude, you can eliminate answer C. Now you've narrowed it down to three choices and considerably increased your chances of guessing right, but you're not done yet.

There's a good chance Edison's name will ring a bell somewhere since he's a rather famous scientist and has his name on all those light bulbs and electric light companies and whatnot. It's also pretty likely that a guy who was so busy inventing electricity and building light bulb factories all over the place didn't have time to go around fathering countries on the side, so you can safely eliminate him, too.

That means you have only two names left and even if you still don't have the faintest idea which one is right at least you've narrowed the choice down to 50/50 and turned the whole thing into another true-false test.

So there you have it. Understanding these basic exams will help you to be one of the survivors and get the hell out of high school alive.

NB - Science tests where they ask you to identify two hundred different chemicals or math tests where you have to work out intricate problems to arrive at an answer are another matter altogether and require extreme measures.

## Chapter Three

### Grades

It's true what they say, that the world really does run on bullshit, and grades are a part of all that. Nobody is interested in talent or ability or potential in the real world; all they care about is the appearance of these traits. People want things to be as they think they are, and they're willing to believe that things are actually as they perceive them to be.

How do you think that dippy girl in the first row with the incredibly short skirts and excellent boobs manages to get A's and B's when she can hardly tell you what page you're on? And what about the star halfback who needs help in finding his way to school every day?

How does that ignorant clod manage to stay eligible for the team unless somebody's bending the rules for him somewhere? Everybody pays lip service to all the clichés about hard work and integrity and discipline and rewarding excellence and the rest of that crap, but watch how they deal with these things in their own lives.

We're a society of hypocrites and four-flushers and humbugs, and it will stand you in good stead if you know that early on. We seldom reward excellence; we always reward bullshit.

Make no mistake about it, though; your grades will count. A high GPA (grade point average) will have a lot to do with your future—or lack thereof. Colleges will depend largely on these GPAs when you apply for admission; in fact, a high GPA can do much to overcome poor SAT or ACT scores. In short, you know you need good grades but the question is what can you do to assure yourself of coming up with them without actually turning into a nerd by studying and really learning something?

On the other hand, a low GPA will be decried by one and all, and no major college or university will consider you. You'll be finished at eighteen, one of life's millions of losers before you really got started, and all because you didn't play by the rules of the game.

Those rules say you need a 2.0 or better to get that diploma so you must come up with that C average no matter what. No one cares how you get it; just see that you have it when you graduate. I've analyzed the problem and come up with some suggestions that will help you pull it off even if you're a less than auspicious student.

So how do you raise your GPA? Take easy courses. Everybody knows you have to work your ass off to get a C in calculus, but you can get an A in wood shop just by learning how to identify two different pieces of lumber, for God's sake. And an A in wood shop is worth twice as many honor points as that C in calculus.

Why, a guy who takes four years of wood shop could have a GPA of 4.0 and go to Harvard while the other guy taking hard courses like calculus could end up with a

GPA of 2.2 and have to join the army just to get a job.

The jocks have known this for years. They go through school taking the easiest courses available and every damn one of them goes on to our finest universities on scholarship. They stay in college long enough to play four years of football and then, forgetting all those years spent in phys ed classes and remedial English, file lawsuits against the school because they can't read. But that's the American way, isn't it?

And remember, who lets them get away with this crap? The very same people who are telling you we reward excellence, that's who. If you can come away with this one concept after reading this book, your money will have been well spent.

Whatever you do, avoid the so-called honors classes. At Cody, if we found out a student could read we'd slap his ass into an honors course where the work is accelerated to challenge the better students. The poor bastard works like a beaver all semester and ends up with a C that could easily have been an A in a regular course.

That's plain silly. While your friends are cruising through senior English with A's you're barely passing the honors classes they conned you into taking. And nobody cares that you took the honors classes; all they see is that glaring 1.8 GPA and somebody sticks a shovel in your hand and points you in the direction of the nearest pile of horseshit.

Another gambit is to sign up for those classes

taught by the "easy" teachers mentioned earlier. Every school has hard teachers and easy ones; you want the easy ones. Some teachers give kids credit just for showing up periodically while others demand college level work for a lousy C. Only a fool would prefer the latter. A perceptive kid can raise his GPA by at least 50% merely by choosing his teachers with care.

Start asking questions as soon as you get to high school in your freshman year. Find out which teachers the jocks sign up with. Peek into the different classrooms on your way to the john and see what's going on. If everybody is bent over his desk and frowning and working his ass off you know that's a teacher to avoid.

If, on the other hand, you look in and see paper airplanes sailing around and kids leaning out of the windows and the teacher idly thumbing through an old Playboy you know this is the class for you. Hurry down to your counselor and tell her you want a transfer to Mr. Slott's class at once.

Still another device is the old-fashioned con job. Make your teachers think you're something you aren't, trick them into believing you're a real student with pure motives and a love of learning for its own sake. Above all, let them think you're crazy about whatever it is they're teaching. All teachers are easily won over by kids who show an interest in their own specialty and tend to look on such kids with favor.

I know it's hard to wax enthusiastic over physics, but it will do you much good if you make the physics teacher believe you've loved the subject since you were a small child and have long planned a career in the field and so on. She'll feel kindly disposed toward you even when you can't grasp the basic fundamentals of the stuff and she'll want to give you the best possible grade. It never fails.

It works because it appeals to our vanity; it even worked on Grandpa Ganja. I remember one case where this little sharper showed up in my English class carrying a large unabridged dictionary and a bag full of novels, poetry, and sundry literary impedimenta.

He took a seat right down front and stacked all these books on the floor where I could see them. He took great pains to let me know that he loved reading and wanted nothing more in life than to be an English teacher and even write books of his own.

Naturally, I took a shine to the little charlatan. I figured any kid who loved literature and fine writing as much as I did had to be all right. It turned out he didn't know any more about English than my cat, but he seemed such a well-meaning kid that I was reluctant to flunk him when he came up with a 46% on the final and let him do some extra assignments to make it up.

The next semester I saw him in Corbin's history class. He was sitting right down front and had a complete set of Gibbon's *Decline and Fall of the Roman Empire* stacked up next to his seat. I knew in a flash I'd been had, of course, but it was too late. If Grandpa Ganja can be fooled anybody can.

Anyway, using some of the above tactics could

easily make a whole grade difference in a given course—and that means more honor points.

If you happen to be a comely female student with a male teacher, always sit down front and wear short skirts, the shorter the better. Undo four or five buttons on your blouse and lean over a lot. Let the old codger see enough thigh and boobs and he'll be too confused by the wonder of it all to know what the hell's going on. Every time he goes to grade one of your test papers his mind will be filled with boobs and thighs and he'll raise your grade at least as high as you raised that skirt.

Trust me. This one works as well as anything I've discussed so far.

These are just a few traditional ways to get better grades in school, reliable schemes that have worked over the years, but they may not be enough to save you. I mean, if you do all these things and still have a GPA lower than sea level you'll have to come up with a better plan. And this brings us to still another long practiced dodge used throughout Christendom for centuries: cheating.

## Chapter Four

### Cheating

Since we're concerned here with truth rather than moral balderdash and buncombe, let's take a close look at cheating generally and see what we're dealing with in the real world.

Of course, a lot of people—mostly teachers—think students shouldn't cheat on their exams, and they have some good reasons for thinking so. For one thing if you cheat too much you run the risk of ending up a total ignoramus, but that's a price you should be willing to pay for success in a world that cares for little else.

Others say you shouldn't cheat because it's dishonest but this is the weakest argument of all. Everybody cheats; he just cheats at different things. We all pay the traditional lip service to honesty and strongly recommend it—for others. We teach kids that honesty is a highly desirable commodity in the world when nothing could be further from the truth.

Take another gander at that George Washington and the cherry tree bullshit. Here we have a patent lie routinely fed to little kids everywhere as a fact. It's an apocryphal story from beginning to end and everybody knows it. Washington never cut down any cherry tree with his little ax, and if he did he tried to cast suspicion on a nearby colony of beavers just as you or any sane person would in a similar situation.

This base canard only serves to further reinforce my point: the hypocritical blackguards in the adult world even lie when they're trying to encourage honesty in their kids.

The fact is most people have very little regard for honesty except when it benefits them. We all want to be honest ourselves as long as it isn't inconvenient for us, or our interests. And this includes your teachers.

How many of your teachers are thoroughly honest when they're trying to unload a used-car on some poor unsuspecting sap? Or when they call in sick because they want to go shopping? Or when they report their taxes to the government? They'll lie and cheat in each of these cases and thousands more and still demand honesty and integrity from you.

That's bullshit. I think you should emulate your teachers in all things and do as they do. Look out for your own best interests just as everyone else is doing and you'll be a lot better off for it.

Okay, now that we've examined the issue at great length and found the truth of the matter, let's get on with some tips on how to cheat successfully, raise your GPA, and finally gain admission to Yale or Princeton where all the big-time cheaters go.

**(A) The Wastebasket Caper**

This one is a sure-fire gimmick that works every time. Wait until the end of the day when all the teachers have left the place (about three minutes after the last bell in most cases) and sneak into the teachers' workroom and go through the wastebaskets. Teachers running off tests on the copier inevitably ruin several copies of the thing and toss them into the wastebasket. You pick them out and bingo! You've got an advance copy of the next test and a guaranteed A.

A caveat: don't share the answers with anyone. Remember, you don't want to raise the class average any higher than necessary. Your own A will look even better if everyone else flunks the test.

**(B) Crib Notes**

This is an old and much used method, but one that still works. You just hunt up the answers to some questions you're fairly sure will be on the test and jot them down on your cuff or on some scraps of paper or the back of the guy's shirt in front of you and copy like hell. Be creative. Put answers up on the ceiling and gaze heavenward for inspiration.

You girls can jot notes down on your thighs and just slide your skirts up your legs as you need fresh answers. The main drawback to this method, though, is that male teachers' eyes are naturally drawn to skirts moving upward on pretty legs and you stand a good chance of getting caught.

Besides, if it's a very long test and the skirt gets too high you'll paralyze the minds of all the guys for four rows in every direction and they'll flunk and their girlfriends will beat the crap out of you for being a shameless hussy.

On the other hand, you may get away with this dodge even in a case where the teacher does spot your sliding skirt. Most men would be moved to helpless inaction while they breathlessly watch with heightened interest to see just how high said skirt will eventually rise.

That's why it's often a good idea to jot down some extra unneeded answers 'way up there so as to keep the old guy's hopes alive that he'll see unexpected marvels if he's patient and doesn't do anything stupid like accusing you of cheating. It's almost too easy, isn't it?

**(C) Be A Counselor's Aide**

Another foolproof plan is to volunteer to be a counselor's aide (for your own counselor, of course) and you'll have access to all the records. All you have to do is change all the undesirable grades on your transcript and stick them back in the files. Nobody will be the wiser and you'll probably win a scholarship to the Graduate School of Business at Harvard or Stanford.

I even knew of one guy who dropped out of high school to join the Marines and later managed to get a high school diploma from a school he never attended. He was dating a girl who worked in the office and she just typed out a complete transcript and stuck the thing in the files with the others. If it worked for him it can work for you.

I should add that this guy was a real dope and had to go back in the Marines and never rose above corporal in twenty years. Still, he had a high school diploma even if it didn't do him much good.

Incidentally, I know some people out there will decry such practices as deceitful and counter productive and even loathsome, but rest assured that some of our finest, most respected citizens regularly do exactly the same thing themselves. There's a flourishing trade in phony diplomas sold through so-called diploma mills all across the land. For a fee anyone can acquire a college degree without going anywhere near a real college or taking a single college course.

And guess who buys the majority of these phony diplomas? Ministers, preachers, holy men that's who! Men of the cloth, guys with their collars on backwards along with their scruples, the very same spiritual leaders who spend all their time telling you to be a Christian and morally straight while they send off for phony Doctor of Divinity degrees paid for with money contributed by morally straight parishioners. Why, the very thought of such hypocrisy shocks Grandpa Ganja to his core.

The preachers are not alone, either. Half the résumés sent out in this country contain phony information including non-existent diplomas, false employment records, and exaggerated salary claims. It's a widespread practice in the business community and everybody knows it, so what's the harm in you following suit? I say if it's good enough for your preacher, it's good enough for you, by God. After all, isn't the only thing that matters that famous bottom line?

**(D) Steal the Grade Book**

This plan is brilliant because of its simplicity. You steal the grade book and throw the damn thing away. Without the grade book the teacher will be forced to give everybody at least a passing mark, i.e., a C, and that's a lot better than the F you'd otherwise have.

Sometimes she saves all your test papers and it will be necessary for you to steal them, too, or she'll be able to reconstruct the grade book and give you your just deserts. If the old bat has cleverly recorded her grades somewhere else, it means she's had previous experience with assholes like you and she's taken steps to thwart you. If that's the case, you may have to do the unthinkable and actually study and learn something.

**(E) Spy on Your Neighbors**

When using this scheme be sure to sit next to somebody who knows what the hell's going on. It's foolish to sit next to some bikers or jocks because you'll just end up copying the wrong answers. You want to copy from the Asian guys with thick glasses and calculators hanging from their belts who know what the hell they're doing.

This time-honored scam involves just looking at your neighbor's work and copying the right answers. Of course, you have to use some care here because teachers are always on the alert for this trick. You need to develop a series of shifty, sidelong glances and subtle distractions that will throw her off.

For instance, be quick to take advantage of any commotion that momentarily distracts her. If somebody raises his hand to ask a question you can sneak a peek at your neighbor's paper while the teacher looks at the question raiser. Or have a friend across the room drop a book on a pre-arranged signal and cop an answer when she looks that way. Also be alert for any interruption, as when somebody appears at the door with a message or she has to answer the intercom.

In other words, this device relies mainly on opportunities that present themselves through chance or by design. It's really one of the least satisfactory gambits but one that can work if you're clever enough or if the teacher is afflicted either with very poor eyesight or unusually slow wits.

**(F) Original Ideas**

As always in life, it pays to be creative and original when possible. I knew one kid who had an exam in a first-floor classroom. He sat next to a window, balled up his exam paper, and tossed it to his friends waiting outside with a textbook and notes. They filled in the answers and threw the balled up paper back into the room.

Unfortunately for him, it fell at my feet and I caught them in the act, as it were. Well, I was so impressed with the sheer brilliance of the scheme that I let the kid take the exam over and this time he failed it on his own and joined the shovel brigade where he belonged in the first place.

**(G) Lie**

A good, well thought out lie is always useful,

especially when all is lost without it. Suppose you have a test coming up and you haven't the foggiest idea of what it's all about. There's no chance in the world you can pass the thing and your whole future hangs in the balance. Clearly, this is a situation calling for drastic measures.

Show up for the test. Spend the period doodling and watching all the skirts slide up and down the girls' legs, and when the test is over don't hand in your paper. When the teacher later asks what happened to your test paper (she knows you were there!) you claim you gave it to her and she lost it. Be firm. Refuse to back down. Insist you did it and that she's at fault. If you're persistent enough she'll give in and you'll come up with some sort of compromise grade.

**(H) Mnemonic Devices**

You'll have to actually do some studying for this one but it works and is worth it if you're desperate. Find the answers and come up with a mnemonic device (look it up) and match it up with your answers. You'll end up with a series of letters or numbers or nonsense syllables that will be meaningless by themselves but that will give you clues to the answers they represent.

The nice thing about this is that you can leave it in plain view on your desk since it means nothing by itself. The teacher will never be able to prove it's anything more than doodling so you'll get off scot-free even if caught.

Well, we could go on, of course, but you get the picture and can probably improvise for yourself. The main thing is when you leave high school you want to look good. Nothing else matters.

## Chapter Five

### Counselors

As an American high school student you will necessarily have to deal with someone known as a "counselor." These individuals may be either male or female, but chances are yours will be a cynical old bat that has seen life as it really is and, accordingly, has no hope. Her job is to advise you on all phases of your academic career, provide guidance on career choices, and muck about in your personal life every chance she gets.

Counselors get to be counselors in various ways, not all of them entirely rational. Some become counselors when their nerves finally give out after years of teaching in the classroom, moving directly from a convalescent center into the counseling cubicle. Others are made counselors as punishment for some real or imagined crime perpetrated against the rules of the school board. And, of course, a lot of them are masochists undergoing a form of aversion therapy.

Once selected, counselors undergo highly specialized training before they're sent into battle. They need a wide variety of experiences and background in order to deal with modern high school students one-on-one.

For instance, counselors are trained to detect beer on the breath of a teenager clear across a standard-sized playing field. They also become proficient at running urine tests for marijuana—a job which requires much of their time in many high schools today—and can frequently be seen hurrying through the halls with racks of yellow-hued test tubes in hand.

They must learn to talk would-be jumpers (usually other counselors) down from high ledges, become handwriting experts to spot all the forged absence excuses that stream across their desks all day, and familiarize themselves with all of the students' inalienable constitutional rights so they'll know which ones of them to violate.

They also have to learn how to overpower crazed students driven mad by the system and generally come to grips with the day-to-day operations of the modern American high school and the people who frequent such places.

It's strongly recommended that nascent counselors have actual hands-on experience with mentally deranged individuals since they will doubtless have considerable contact with such people once they hit a real high school and have to contend with the teachers they find there.

Many counselor-trainees have even cleverly disguised themselves as patients and spent months or years in various sanatoriums and psycho wards to get first-hand knowledge of the techniques used in such work. (Some think they weren't phony patients at all, but that's another story.)

Counselors must also be wary of substance abuse—not the kids, I mean their own. The job is so nerve-wracking and riddled with anxiety and tension that the average counselor is almost always on something before long. A lot of them are on the bottle.

Some of them smoke the dope they take from the kids and end up getting hooked on the stuff and have to go into prostitution and crime in order to support their habits. Others are on Valium and speed and uppers and downers and assorted mind-altering drugs and potions required to get them through a day of meeting American teenagers face-to-face in a never-ending battle of wits that the kids always seem to win.

Grandpa Ganja is sympathetic. No wonder they get stoned.

You'll often find counselors located in a counseling center with several other counselors, each of them in a cubicle with walls that don't reach the ceiling. They build them that way to be sure nobody has any privacy, as every word you say can be heard by people in nearby cubicles.

And, what's worse, since your counselor is an old-timer she'll probably have a hearing problem which means you'll have to shout the most intimate things at the top of your voice so the whole damn school will know you've missed your last three periods almost as soon as you know it yourself.

Such a scene might look something like this.

A troubled teenager enters the counseling center and heads for her counselor's cubicle.

"Well, what do *you* want?" Miss Grinde snaps.

The girl sits nervously and looks around apprehensively. "Uh, Miss Grinde, I wanted to see you about..."

"What?!" Miss Grinde says loudly. "Speak up! What are you whispering for? Speak up!"

"Well," the girl says a bit louder, "it's personal and..."

"Are you going to speak up or not?" Miss Grinde shouts in a booming voice. "I haven't got all day, you know! Spit it out, for God's sake!"

Well, the girl is pissed by now and she shouts, "Okay, you old bat! I've missed my last three periods! There! Is that loud enough for you?"

The girl storms out and Miss Grinde shrugs and takes another pinch of snuff before counseling the next guy in line.

I've known kids who tried to avoid a similar experience by writing it all down on a sheet of paper so she could read it to herself, but that doesn't work because counselors are carefully trained to recognize this ploy and deal with it.

Miss Grinde takes a proffered note from a student entering her cubicle.

"What's this?" she booms out. "A note?" She reads it aloud. "Hmmm. You say you missed your period?" The girl winces. Miss Grinde reads on. "What?! You missed three periods!" The girl reddens and tries to hide. "Say, Cindy Jones, just what the hell have you been up to, anyway? Do your folks know about this? I'll have to make out a full report to the student council. You'll probably be expelled and driven from the neighborhood in disgrace!" Etc.

Another victory for the high school counselor over teenage malfeasance.

Counselors also have the responsibility of helping you choose the right courses. When you first arrive as a freshman she'll analyze your profile and determine which courses you're most suited for and then she'll program you into something as far from that as possible.

She'll carefully question you to learn that you can't stand manual labor, hate getting your hands dirty, and dislike all things mechanical, and then the wily old bat will sign you up for a four-year course in auto mechanics and machine shop.

What's worse, once you get locked into a schedule you can't get out of it. You'll have to hire a lawyer and launch a series of court trials to get the thing changed to something you can live with.

Your counselor will also advise you on possible career choices, although you shouldn't place too much confidence in her since she didn't do all that well in choosing a career for herself.

I've seen the following scene enacted too many times.

Kid enters Miss Grinde's cubicle seeking career counseling.

"So you want to be a lawyer, eh?" she says with a sneer.

"Well, I thought..." the kid starts to say.

"Are you kidding?" Miss Grinde snaps. "With your record you'll be needing a good lawyer before you can ever become one yourself!" She riffles through her files. "You aren't on suspension, are you?" she demands suspiciously.

"No, Miss Grinde, I..." the kid says.

"Look," she says, "why don't you forget this lawyer stuff and just sign up for another year of auto mechanics? They always need good mechanics, you know."

"But I..."

"Just sign right here under auto mechanics. That's right. See? Wasn't that easy?" She calls out. "Okay, next!"

The kid is on his way back to the auto shop and the dedicated counselor has successfully saved still another student from taking up a life of crime and rapine. Now that's what high school counseling is all about, by God!

## Chapter Six

### Teachers, Wanton

A warning: you young guys need to be on the lookout for certain amoral young lady teachers who manage to infiltrate our schools and prey on the students. They're a very real threat in schools everywhere, one that could undermine your moral fiber and turn you all into a bunch of sex-starved guys who spend all their time trying to get laid and drinking beer and ignoring those things of real value like hard work and strict discipline and self-denial.

You know the ones I mean. They're usually young and have great boobs and long, slim legs and a look in their eye that would arouse carnal thoughts in a holy man, for God's sake. They never wear bras. They wear blouses that gape wide open so when they bend over some poor slob's desk to help him with his work their boobs swing back and forth and bump together like a couple of ripe melons and hypnotize his ass.

I've seen it happen many times: two or three slow, majestic swings to and fro are enough to paralyze the average teenager's mind completely and leave him vulnerable to the most unspeakable delights, er, dangers.

I've often seen these wanton hussies sit on top of the teacher's desk while leading discussions with their skirts sliding heavenward and exposing enough thighs to alarm a lot of retired eunuchs. They cross and recross their nylon-clad legs and provide brief visual flashes of the most marvelous sights imaginable. Every poor sap in the room is mentally transfixed, of course, and overpowered by primal urges not to be denied by healthy young men—or semi-healthy older men, for that matter.

Naturally, you guys aren't able to concentrate on your studies with that display going on. The only thing in the room you can focus your attention on isn't going to be on the test. It's a basic law of nature that the grades of guys in such a class will fall in direct proportion to the rise of other things.

Well, I say you guys out there shouldn't stand for it! (In point of fact, it's not a good idea to stand at all if you can possibly avoid it for obvious reasons—or reasons that will be pretty obvious if you do stand.) These teachers have no right to exhibit themselves in this way and drive you poor bastards nuts with bizarre, sex-filled fantasies and desperate longings to be kept after school like the lucky clown in the famous teacher-keeps-the-kid-after-school-story we all know and love. Don't stand for it, I say!

We've got to rid our schools of these crazed sexpot nymphomaniacs before it's too late. In fact, I've already declared open war on them; I've launched a campaign to drive these vixens the hell out of our schools. I'll meet them one-on-one and straighten the lot of them out one at a time or bunched in groups if that's what it takes.

But I need your help. If you know of any of these wanton, sex-crazed teachers in your school, let me know at once. Forward their names, addresses, and phone numbers (and a picture so I'll know them when I see them) and leave the rest to me. I've seen these types come and go in my time and I know what to do with 'em.

You can trust Grandpa Ganja on that, by God.

## Chapter Seven

### Classroom Seating

It's very important that you choose the right seat in your classes since that decision can have a strong bearing on whether you pass or fail a given class. Only the most naive kids just stroll in and sit any old place; the smart ones plan ahead.

Never sit in the very last row in any case because all teachers know that's where the assholes gather. When a kid enters a room for the first time and heads for the last row of seats, the teacher automatically marks his name down in her record book with the notation "asshole" beside it. Needless to say, such a kid starts out with two strikes against him in that class.

Check it out. Look at the kids sitting in the last row in your classes and whom do you see back there? No-Neck Knudsen from the football squad; Bojangles Smith, reefer salesman; Arnie Wamp, professional truant, et al.

These guys sit in the back because they mistakenly believe they're less likely to be called on back there. The truth is these are the very people the teacher immediately zeroes in on and watches with an eye jaundiced by years of experience with others like them.

If a spitball sails across the room, the teacher instantly looks to the back row. The guy who shot it may be sitting right in front of her, but she'll look to the back row every time. It's a matter of conditioning. Experience has taught her that this is where the troublemakers are to be found, and that's where she looks. Well, don't let yourself be found among them.

On the other hand, it's dangerous to sit smack in front of the old bat because you become too easy a target. I mean, sometimes a certain measure of boldness is called for, but you don't want to be stupid about it. If you're in the very front seats it's almost impossible to avoid eye contact with the teacher, and it's eye contact that'll get your ass in trouble every time.

After all, the one thing most high school kids want to avoid is being called on to recite in class so their ignorance will be exposed to the entire world five or six times a day. It's bad enough when you look like a complete dope once in a while, but nobody wants it on a regular basis.

Teachers call on kids who catch their eye, and that's why it's a good rule never to look directly at the teacher. When she's peering about for a likely target you fix your gaze on your textbook and frown mightily as though engrossed by some particularly obscure fact therein, or look busily through your book bag, or take notes furiously, but whatever you do don't let the old biddy catch your eye. You're a goner if she does, and that's why you need to avoid the very front rows.

If you happen to be a real student who actually does some work once in a while and aren't terrified of being called on because you know the answers, then the front row is perfect. Teachers tend to look on kids sitting down front as better students and less overall trouble, but the benefits gained by sitting there are offset by the danger of being shown up as an academic lout every fifteen minutes.

Seats along the sides are not too good, either, because you're also somewhat exposed there. Teachers are trained in teacher colleges to keep a close watch on the back rows and both sides to protect their flanks from a surprise attack. The one advantage to a side seat is you can be close to a window and have something to look at to relieve the incredible boredom, a fact which may make it worth the added risk of sitting in an exposed position.

This leaves the center section where the smart kids sit. You blend right in with those around you and do nothing to attract attention. Try not to stand out by being the only white kid in a cluster of black kids (or vice-versa), or the only atheist in a herd of born-again Christians, or the only guy with a lot of girls on all sides.

The Marines taught Grandpa Ganja that motion attracts notice so try to avoid any more moving about than absolutely necessary. Sit behind a big kid, one who weighs three- or four-hundred-pounds, if possible. Slump down in your seat. The chances are the teacher's eyes will slide right over your motionless form and light on some asshole in the back row who's flapping around in his seat saying, "Hey, look at me!"

With a little luck and a lot of planning, you may

go through your entire high school career without ever once having your astonishing ignorance broadcast throughout the school.

    NB - These rules will vary somewhat depending on the circumstances. For instance, if the teacher is known to have a severe vision problem and can't see more than three rows back, you can obviously sit anywhere except the first three rows. You may adjust accordingly if the teacher is totally deranged and completely unpredictable, or if he (she) is known to be partial to good-looking girls (boys) or displays some other idiosyncrasy that calls for adapting on your part.

    In any case, get there early on the first day and grab one of those four or five key seats. This maneuver alone could add a whole point to your GPA over four years of high school and help make you one of the survivors.

# Chapter Eight

### Clubs

There are clubs of various kinds that you may join in all modern high schools worthy of the name, but it's important that you use some care in choosing one. First, of course, you'll have to find one that will accept you as a member, a task that may not be all that easy for a lot of you.

Before you can make an intelligent choice among the many different clubs available, you'll need to know which of them will most nearly meet your own needs and what requirements will have to be met on your part. I mean, you'd be making a serious mistake if you went blindly ahead and joined the Chess Club when you have an IQ of eighty-five and a twenty-two-inch neck. It's obvious you'd be more suited to the Future Coaches Club, isn't it?

Let's consider some of the more popular clubs found in our high schools these days and outline some of their outstanding characteristics and salient features and see if one or more of them will appeal to you.

**(A) Motorcycle Clubs**

What the hell, let's start at the bottom with clubs composed entirely of leather-clad louts with IQs in the moronic range. We know their IQs are low because only the slow-witted will ride the freeways at 80 mph in a car without seatbelts or air bags or even a roof, for Christ's sake. Anyway, biker clubs have very stringent requirements for new members, requirements not easily met by the average American teenager, fortunately.

For one thing, you must be unclean in mind, spirit, and, especially, body. It's the number one requirement of the organization and is contained in every club's charter issued by the parent organization, International Assholes, Inc. These guys wash their bikes more often than they do themselves, never change their underwear (if they even wear any), and are unacquainted with combs, toothbrushes, deodorant, and good manners.

Motorcycle clubs are almost entirely male with the few female members being largely indistinguishable from the guys. This is a moot point, of course, since no refined, urbane teenage kid would look for romance in a biker club in the first place.

Potential members must hate learning in all its forms and agree to cover themselves with ugly tattoos. A limited vocabulary is highly regarded in these circles and sub-standard English is the norm. You should have your own motorcycle, of course, and it should be a Harley.

Motorcycle people like fistfighting, all kinds of drugs, beer, riding their bikes, and nooky—probably in that order.

**(B) Jock Clubs**

These clubs are a cut above motorcycle clubs, but not much above them. Jocks do bathe occasionally and some of them have been known to change their underwear now and then. To belong to a jock club you'll need the above-mentioned twenty-two-inch neck and an IQ somewhere in the high eighties. If your IQ is any higher than this you'll be smarter than the coach and that will piss him off. Some jocks will have a larger neck size than IQ and these guys are usually the leaders by unanimous consent.

To be a jock it's also useful if you play a sport of some kind, preferably a major one like football or baseball or basketball, but even a second-stringer on the tennis or swim team can qualify. The important thing is to hang out in the gym and do all the things the other jocks do so people can identify you as one of them. A letter sweater helps. So does a limited vocabulary, though it doesn't have to be as limited as that of the bikers.

It goes without saying that you must love sports above all else. Jocks must invest heavily in baseball gloves, hockey sticks, bats, tennis racquets, sneakers, and liniment. These guys are keenly interested in balls of all kinds including the ones found on the male anatomy. They often speak of having balls as a macho thing. If you are said to be without balls you will be lightly regarded by jocks everywhere—and even more lightly regarded by girls who know intuitively nothing can be done with such a guy.

Since jocks spend a lot of time hanging around gyms and locker rooms, it helps if you either have no sense of smell at all or a well-developed dirty sweat sock fetish to accommodate the indelicate aromas found in such places. They say you get used to it but why would you want to?

For quicker acceptance in the locker room, learn some of the colorful phrases jocks use in praise of macho ideals like, "The going gets tougher when the tough get going!" and "Give 110%!" and "Up yours!" and similar clichés. Remember to be monosyllabic.

Jocks like sports, beer, comic books, steroids, and nooky.

**(C) Academic Clubs**

This heading includes science, Latin, math, and similar clubs devoted to intellectual things and dullness. Members of these clubs wear glasses, understand calculus, and go to bed (alone) every night at nine. They are always former Scouts and have collections of butterflies pinned on large sheets of cardboard. These guys always have high IQs accompanied by practically no social sense, so they're the last ones called for proms, big frat parties, and orgies.

Academic clubs usually have formal meetings using Robert's Rules of Order. They often invite favorite teachers as guest speakers. And everybody picks on them because they're wimps. Once at Cody one of the motorcycle guys disguised himself by taking a bath and slipped unnoticed into a meeting of the science club. Some poor sap was showing off his collection of North American arachnids and the biker ate them.

Science club types like total eclipses, equations,

homework, and computers. Most of them haven't found out about girls/boys yet.

**(D) Fraternities/Sororities**

These clubs are made up of teenage yuppies and other upwardly bound types who frown on synthetic fabrics and wouldn't be caught dead in a shop class. They regard themselves as superior to their classmates and they conduct themselves accordingly. Nobody likes them.

They value material things such as clothes, cars, and money. Most of them have none of these things themselves, of course, but they come from affluent homes where such things are provided them absolutely without cost. Naturally, it never occurs to them that they're living on handouts, that somebody else had to go out and hustle to come up with the scratch to buy these goodies. They like to think they somehow earned their BMWs all by themselves, but everybody else knows the real truth and regards them with contempt—and envy, too.

Fraternities, like motorcycle clubs, have very stringent requirements for new members, i.e., you have to prove you're an asshole here, too. Once accepted, though, you'll learn the secret handshake used by yuppies everywhere and be admitted into their innermost circles.

This is not merely an empty honor, I might add. These clubs have a well-founded reputation for keeping files of old exams that are made available to all members in good standing. They usually have any given exam six months in advance, and that's time enough for even a yuppie to find the answers and jot them down in his palm. This technique enables them to get into those Ivy League colleges they covet so much where they quickly join new fraternities so they can get the answers to the exams there.

Sororities are nothing more complicated than fraternities for girls.

Frat guys like beer, cars, marijuana, and chicks. Sorority girls like clothes, vicious gossip, and frat guys.

**(E) Miscellaneous Clubs**

Other clubs you might find in the average American high school could include chess clubs, Bible clubs, future teachers clubs, rod and gun clubs (in Detroit, anyway), and assorted fringe groups made up of people unable to get into any of the mainstream clubs listed above. Avoid them. They're for losers and rejects and will further damage your social life—if such a thing is possible.

You see, if you show up in one of these losers' clubs everybody will know you're a joiner who would like to be in a major club but didn't have what it takes. On the other hand, a refusal to join any club indicates contempt for the whole club mentality and actually implies superiority since you consider such organizations beneath you. Ergo: you don't join any of them.

And that's Grandpa Ganja's final advice: avoid all clubs. People with real class remain aloof from such nonsense; they don't need the approval of others to feel confidence in themselves and sure of their place in the world. Why submit to the ignominious shame of "...trying to tease out a smile on some cold face..." as Cyrano put it so elegantly in the play? Why let a lot of ignorant assholes vote on whether you're an acceptable companion or not?

Remember Groucho Marx's famous remark: "I wouldn't belong to any club that would have me as a member."

If that's good enough for Groucho, it's good enough for you.

## Chapter Nine

### GYM

Everybody hates gym—except jocks, of course, and they don't count. For most kids gym is a real drag. There are a lot of reasons for this and one of them is because all gyms smell like swamps, as we just saw. I can still remember entering a gym for the first time and looking around for the alligators I knew had to be somewhere nearby.

The smell carries for great distances, too. When I walked past the open gym doors at Cody I always took a big breath and tried not to breathe again until I was far enough down the hall to be out of range, a distance of several hundred feet at the very least.

These gym odors sink into a person's persona after sufficient exposure and are well nigh impossible to get rid of. I've known old coaches retired after decades in the fetid air of high school gyms that were enveloped in nearly visible clouds of locker room air, its less than delicate aromas embedded in their very skin and character. It's not a pleasant sight or smell.

Some scientists recently concluded that the smell of sweat is an aphrodisiac and the perfume industry is selling it to saps everywhere. Hell, all you have to do is bottle the air in the average gym and you could turn on every virgin in the senior class—if you could find any.

To this day I dislike exercise because the stuff smells so bad.

Kids hate gym for other reasons than the smell, though. Girls hate it because they don't like getting their hair wet in the pool or shower. They also hate it because they don't like to be seen naked in the shower by their classmates. High school girls have this thing about being seen naked, but something happens to them after graduation and they start appearing in porno flicks or entering wet T-shirt contests all over town. So much for this false modesty bullshit.

Guys, on the other hand, don't give a damn who sees them naked. They'll wander all over the locker room in the buff and snap wet towels at each other and never give it a thought. In fact, a lot of guys are so indifferent to being seen naked that they eventually end up running around town in trench coats and little else and have to make occasional court appearances as a result. And they don't care if their hair gets wet, either.

Another reason kids don't like gym is they make you do dumb things there. Take rope climbing, for instance. Who needs to be able to shinny up a rope unless he's planning a career as a burglar, for God's sake? Or who wants to spend an entire gym period doing calisthenics? Most kids aren't all that enthused about deep-knee bends or doing jumping jacks all over the place.

Besides, I can't think of anything dumber than making a roomful of teenagers do calisthenics in the first place. They don't need exercise; if anybody needs it, it's the coaches. These guys are sorry advertisements for the product they're selling, i.e., good health. Most of them have physiques resembling fat sausages. They toss out a few basketballs, sound a single blast on their whistles, and wheeze for the next quarter-of-an-hour.

Talk about role models; these guys give gym a bad name. Kids are afraid if they exercise they'll end up looking like their coaches, and that's not a pleasant prospect for your average reed-thin and swiftly moving American teenager. If a kid turns out to look like his coach, his parents should sue for educational malpractice.

Lady gym teachers don't fare much better, I hasten to add. The only thing I ever saw them exercising was their elbows in the gym office where they spent the day downing jelly doughnuts and coffee.

Actually, the real reason they make you take gym in high school is so you'll burn up all your excess energy doing calisthenics and have less of it to use in getting laid. Hard, prolonged exercise will drive impure thoughts completely out of your mind—another reason I don't like it. The way I see it everybody has just so much energy and he can use it up doing calisthenics or jogging or making out. Most high school kids realize this and make the appropriate choice.

The secret is to conserve all the energy you can during gym and you'll have enough left over to score with your favorite partner(s) several times a week.

Always play guard in basketball games because guards don't do as much running as forwards and centers. Always be the last one in line for rope climbing and the period will usually end before they get to you.

When in the pool pretend you can't swim and the coach will let you splash around in the shallow end and you'll use up almost no energy at all. Cheat in cross-country runs. Stride briskly to the first turn and then duck out and head back to the parking lot where you can rest and catch a smoke or something until the jocks get back entirely bereft of energy.

Be sure to get eliminated in the first round of every tennis match, track event, ping-pong tournament, or what have you and you'll have enough excess energy to straighten out the entire cheerleading team—or backfield, depending on your gender and preferences.

A word regarding exercise after high school: don't. More old duffers (guys in their thirties, even) are struck down in a given year by heart attacks and strokes brought on by careless exercise than are lost to smoking cigars, drinking beer, and philandering combined. A good brisk walk from the couch to the refrigerator for another beer is more than enough exercise for any man. Exercise will only make you tired and, as Mark Twain said, there isn't any advantage in that.

So don't be conned into joining a lot of so-called health clubs, aerobics classes, bike marathons, and similar nonsense. You don't want to end up in one of those little stories tucked away in the middle of the local paper wherein they describe how some clown was found on the sidewalk clad in a jogging suit and deader than a mackerel with an astonished look on his mug. Can anything be more ironic?

Anyway, follow the above advice and conserve those "vital juices" for the ultimate athletic event—and if you don't know what that is go ahead and sign up for the next Boston Marathon.

It's obvious that anything as unappealing as gym has to be avoided at all costs. How does one go about doing that? Easy. Just get a note from your doctor saying you have a heart murmur and should spend the gym period lying down somewhere. Hold your hand over your heart and gasp for air when you hand the note over. It works like a charm.

Why, I've seen times when half the kids at Cody were critical heart patients just a beat away from multiple bypass surgery, and the coaches were afraid to challenge them since they feared lawsuits in case they were telling the truth and fell over dead on the gym floor.

Girls can have four or five periods a month—or claim to. When the coach demands to know why the hell you aren't out there beating the crap out of the other girls with a field-hockey stick, you declare there's nothing you'd rather be doing but it's, uh, you know, uh, and trail off aimlessly. The big sap will be embarrassed by the whole thing and anxious to bring the conversation to a halt. He'll nod knowingly and tell you to go sit in the bleachers and you'll have avoided gym for still another time.

One ruse that works well is to tell them you can't dress for gym because your gym clothes are being washed. I don't know why the coach buys this one since he knows damn well nobody ever washes his gym clothes, but he will. You can throw your things away and say somebody stole them. If you go to school in Detroit you won't be lying on this one since they steal everything in this burg.

Limp and tell him you tore a ligament while practicing for the pentathlon. Smoke a joint before gym class and tell the fathead you don't give a damn about him or any of his simian relations, either. Polish off a six-pack in the parking lot and throw up on the coach's shoes.

Any of these devices will get you out of your gym class, and a couple of them will put you in the infirmary with multiple injuries. Still, if it gets his ass out of gym, the average high school kid will consider it worth the price.

Remember, keep your hair dry and store up those vital juices.

## Chapter Ten

### Truancy

Every normal American high school student cuts classes at least once in a while; in fact, I have no use for a kid with a perfect attendance record. I always figure the little schemer is up to no good and keep a close watch on him to make sure he doesn't do anything irregular.

It's true. Perfect attendance isn't normal behavior anywhere. The kid who shows up with a shotgun and decimates his English class one day is always the same kid who goes to church four or five times a week, is an Eagle Scout, and has perfect attendance since kindergarten. Never trust such people.

Fortunately, such kids are rare indeed. The large majority of high school kids today play hooky every chance they get and, accordingly, need all the help they can get in avoiding detection. This section is aimed at providing assorted ways to deal with your own truancy, inside information garnered from thirty years of handling hooky players of every race, creed, and political persuasion.

Of course, things have changed somewhat over the years. When I was in high school we played hooky to get away from the place. We went to a nearby pool hall or hung out in a hamburger joint and smoked cigarettes and generally tried to put the time to some good use, but today kids at Cody are what we called in-school truants; the bastards cut class and never leave the building.

Out of three-thousand kids in the school we had only about two-thirds of them in class at a time while the other thousand were running all over the place hiding in doorways, setting fires, and pissing in the stairwells. Everybody knew who these guys were, of course, and we rounded them up periodically and expelled two or three truckloads of them, but the school board made us take them right back and the game went on to everybody's chagrin.

Well, assuming you are one of the more rational hooky players and interested in getting away with it insofar as that's possible, the following ideas are submitted for your consideration. One or more of these schemes is bound to work if you follow instructions carefully.

For openers, when you report back to school after cutting class always remember to check whether the teacher was absent the same day you were. If you find out she was absent too you just lie and swear you were there and the sub made a mistake. Call on a friend for corroboration; you lie and he'll swear to it. This will raise some uncertainty in the teacher's mind and she'll be forced to give you the benefit of the doubt.

Or tell the teacher you forgot your absence excuse but you'll bring it in tomorrow for sure. Tell her this every day as long as you can get away with it. Some teachers will let you slide forever.

Steal the teacher's roll book and burn it to hide

the evidence. However, this dodge won't work where they use computers since all the records will be on tape somewhere. You'll have to steal the tapes, and while you're at it you may as well steal the computers, too.

If you can steal the teacher's seating chart and erase your name from it, you won't have to show up for the rest of the semester. Also, remember to check the mail at your house every day before your parents see it and throw out all mail coming from the school. It isn't even necessary to read the stuff; if it's from the school it can't be good news. Just throw it out.

Some kids take more esoteric approaches to covering their truancy tracks. We had one guy at Cody who broke into our computer system and printed up a four-year perfect attendance record for himself on the damn thing. Not only that but the nervy bastard also gave himself a high school diploma with an all-A average, left the building and never came back. We caught him four years later when he showed up for graduation to get his diploma and nobody knew who the hell he was.

The backbone of any successful hooky-playing program is, of course, the well-written absence excuse. Ideally, you should start no later than the first-grade the very first time you're absent and your mother writes an absence excuse for you. Throw that first note away, write it again yourself, and sign your mother's name. That way the school will have your handwriting on file right from the start and you can safely write your own excuses for the rest of your academic career.

If you didn't have the foresight to do that in the first-grade, the least you can do is forge the first absence excuse you put on file in high school, as there is little real communication between the schools and they'll probably never know the difference.

One caveat here: be sure you can spell your mother's name. Even the slower teachers get suspicious when her name is Elaine and you spell it Elane.

As with other excuses, you should be creative and original when coming up with absence notes. If your teacher happens to have a religious bent and is known to consort with Bible thumpers, make a point of carrying a Bible around with you, one of those thirty-pound jobs with colored ribbons hanging out of all the places you've marked out for memorizing, and show up after ten days' absence with a cast on your elbow. Tell the teacher you fell off a ladder while helping the deacon paint the church. What Christian could doubt a story like that?

As for the written note itself, there are some things to remember. For one, be bold. Always include your home phone number. It's a nice touch and it lends an air of authenticity to the fraud. After all, would a guilt-ridden hooky player have the balls to dangle that tempting phone number right in front of the teacher's nose like that?

Damn right if he's a survivor.

Be brief. Mothers don't write long letters to tell some NFL reject why their kids missed gym class, for Christ's sake. A line or two is enough. Remember, all you want to do is cover your ass, not start a relationship between your mother and some bozo in the locker room.

A good, well-written absence excuse might look something like this.

Miss Shrill: 2-14

Please excuse Calvin's absence yesterday. He had a dental appointment. Please call me at 555-1212 if there are any questions.

Mrs. Jane Smith

There. Short and to the point, nothing subtle about it. Most teachers would accept it at face value in a minute. I'd accept the damn thing myself, and have a thousand times—unless I find I'm dealing with a professional hooky player, a guy who makes his living skipping school.

This is the kid who's out more than he's in, the guy whose name you never learn because you never see him often enough to find out who the hell he is. He skips school in all weather and for no particular reason. He likes the challenge. And, because he never goes to any of his classes, he's always an ignorant asshole.

We have whole schools full of these guys in Detroit. They're real pros, the best in the business. Most of them can't read a whole sentence in a row without getting lost, but you'd swear they were all Harvard Law School graduates when you try to hang a truancy rap on them. They're familiar with every existing law on the books dealing with truancy and they make up new ones as they go along.

They're ingenious as hell, too. Instead of claiming their grandmother died (a real cliché in the absence excuse trade), they'll claim the whole family was wiped out and they had to attend funerals in four different states and that's why they haven't been in school for the last month.

These guys always include the phone number but it's always a phony number. They never live where the records say they do, either. In fact, a lot of them are actually nomads and have no real homes that you can actually find anywhere. And they write absence notes that would fool P. T. Barnum himself.

Consider the following gem from one of these guys.

Dr. Keliher:                                           2-14
Derrick was absent yesterday because our house burned down. He stayed home to help us look thru the ashes for our furniture. You can call me at my sister's where we're staying. 555-1212.

Mrs. Jane Smith

Nicely done, but the real beauty of this note lies in the fact that it was written on the back of an old envelope that was actually water marked and singed around the edges! I knew the note was a phony at once, of course, but I accepted it immediately as a tribute to the skill of a master craftsman and gave the crooked little forger a clean bill of health for the entire month. It was the least I could do.

Well, there you have it. A quick analysis of hooky playing in the modern American high school including a few useful dodges to help you pull the wool over their eyes when you just can't face another period of world history to save your ass.

It's amazing how much more interesting the average pool hall or hamburger joint is.

## Chapter Eleven

### Holdups

While the average high school student in more or less civilized localities may not have much use for advice on how to deal with holdups, the ones living in Detroit and other large urban areas will appreciate its value. This burg has a surfeit of losers and half-wits who are armed to the teeth and specialize in sticking-up teenagers for their Nike sneakers, "ropes" (gold chains), bomber jackets, and the odd lunch money.

These robberies often take place when the victim is on the way to or from school. (It's also possible in Detroit to be held up at gunpoint in the school itself but cops permanently stationed in each school discourage such activity on the whole.) The usual practice is for three or four ugly guys—these guys are always ugly—to pull to the curb and call the victim over under the pretense of asking directions or some similar ruse. When you approach the car they stick a gun in your face and demand your sneakers, etc.

If this should happen to you, feign innocence and take a step toward them to allay suspicion and then turn and run like hell in the opposite direction so they'll have to turn the car around to chase you. Nine times out of ten they'll just drive off and look for another victim who's less fleet of foot.

The tenth time they'll leap out and open fire on

your fleeing ass and maybe put a bullet through an arm or leg and drop you in your tracks. In that case, you'll probably lose your sneakers.

On the other hand, if the robbers get the drop on you at close range, the experienced holdup victim (you) should throw your hands up in the classic pose of the robbee everywhere and commence begging and pleading for your life even as you struggle to untie those sneakers and hand them over.

In fact, cooperation is the watchword here. Give the guy anything he wants. Tell him where he can find friends of yours wearing even better sneakers than your own. Suggest possible escape routes for his use after he's finished robbing you. Offer to hold his gun for him while he packs your stuff in a box. In short, don't give the bastard any reason to shoot you.

Remember, you're dealing with a real ignoramus here, a dude with an IQ on a par with the average jackass, and you'll be lucky if the asshole doesn't shoot you just to see if his gun is in working order.

Another tactic to guard against robbers is to have a large caliber pistol of your own in your book bag and when the bastards pull up and ask for directions whip it out and spray them with bullets. You'll usually catch them by surprise and will be able to plug two or three of them before they know what's going on. If you're a good enough shot you'll incapacitate the whole lot of them and you can then take their sneakers and ropes and teach them a valuable lesson at the same time.

Of course, if they happen to be innocent guys

who really do just want directions, you'll have to answer to the police for winging citizens without sufficient provocation. Still, in Detroit that won't be much of a problem since the jails are too full to hold any more crooks and you'll just get a stern warning and a few months probation.

Anyway, if you run into these dudes and you do manage to escape with your life you're a survivor. You will live to be robbed again—and probably will be if you stay in Motown for long.

## Chapter Twelve

### Johns

Most high school kids think the school johns are much more interesting than their classes, a fact which explains why so many of them find it necessary to visit one six or seven times a day. The first hand raised in every class period is a kid asking for a pass to the john.

This is especially true in Detroit schools where the average school john will hold up to a hundred or more thugs, dopers, hooky players, and ne'er-do-wells at a time and is always so jammed that one must make reservations days in advance before stopping by to take a leak.

The reason these johns are so popular is because these places are the hubs of social activity in most high schools. It's here you find the best (or worst, depending on your point of view) kids in the school who come together to form a united front against the incredible boredom of the place.

The john is where the dope dealers and smokers congregate, though it's not always easy to see them in the clouds of smoke. These guys are always entertaining, especially if you stay long enough to inhale a quart or two of the smoke-filled air. After a few deep breaths you'll notice everyone is grinning at you. A few more breaths and you'll be grinning back.

These places are always crowded because

everybody goes there but nobody ever comes back. I gave a kid a pass to the john on Monday and didn't see him again until Thursday. I think he spent the whole time in that john. You'll have to get there early in the day if you want a seat, a concern of special interest to girls. Some kids are permanent residents and get their mail there. A john in a Detroit school recently burned down and left five hundred homeless.

High school johns can also be unsafe because thugs hang out in them. When the average thug enters a school he usually heads straight for the john so he can be with others of his own kind. It's a good place to lose your lunch money or gold chains or even some teeth. Some kids find the johns so scary they never go in them at all, which may explain why so many kids are pissing in the stairwells at Cody.

Various things are bought and sold in high school johns. Besides the aforementioned dope, you can buy answers to exams, recently stolen textbooks to replace the ones recently stolen from you, condoms (new and used), a set of very recently used tires, and similar items usually popular with teenagers. It's a remarkable example of the free enterprise system at work and should inspire greedy bastards everywhere.

Still, in order to keep on top of things, I volunteered to conduct an on-the-spot investigation of the johns in our school to learn whether organized crime was involved in them. The plan was for me to hide out in one of the johns and take notes on what went on in there.

I got there at dawn before the place began filling up, hung an out-of-order sign on a stall door, and hid inside with my note pad at the ready. The first kids to arrive began making coffee and setting up their dope displays. A three-piece combo tuned up in one corner as the early shift began arriving.

The following is a verbatim account of what I heard.

"Hey, Benny, where you pos' to be?"

"I got history first hour, man."

"History? Shit, no wonder you in here."

"Yeah. That stuff is really borin'. Puts me right to sleep."

"You right, man. They should put that shit up in bottles. They could put sleeping pills out of business in a minute. Here, take a hit of this. You can make your own history, man."

He must have given Benny something to smoke because a lot of smoke started seeping into my stall. I wrote furiously. Another voice called out, an angry one.

"Hey, man, you pissin' on my shoe!"

"Well, you standin' in the urinal, asshole!"

"Oh, yeah?"

Sounds of a scuffle and shouts rang out. More smoke seeped in and I wrote on. Another voice.

"Who got a cigarette?"

"What kind? Tobacco or dope?"

"Gimme the dope, man. That tobacco shit can give your ass cancer."

More smoke, other voices.

"What time do the second hour start?"

"How much you want for that carburetor, man?"

"So I tol' the motherfucker, 'Look, motherfucker, I ain't playin,' I goes..."

"Did you see the boobs on that girl, man?"

A bell rang somewhere and there was a lot of commotion and noise and more smoke poured into my stall and then everything went blank. The principal organized a raiding party and they broke in and found me at lunchtime. I had been overcome by the dreaded marijuana smoke and lost touch with reality—a not altogether unpleasant experience with reality being what it is, I might add.

I had emerged from the stall and was leading a group of louts in a discussion on the merits of the Protestant work ethic as opposed to a life devoted to anarchy and good times when the raiding party saved me from myself and led me to safety.

While my investigation couldn't exactly be called a complete success, at least we determined organized crime wasn't involved in our johns. We should have expected that, of course, since the last thing you'd ever find in one of Detroit's schools is organization of any kind.

So there you have an overview of life as it's known in high school johns in modern America. My advice is to avoid them, but if you do have to go tell them Grandpa Ganja sent you—and make sure some asshole isn't standing in the urinal.

## Chapter Thirteen

### SUMMER SCHOOL

Everybody hates summer school. The kids hate it because it's always hotter than a bitch and boring beyond belief. The teachers hate it for the same reasons. Scientists say time can actually slow down; hell, any kid who ever sat through a summer school class in world history would tell them it can come to a dead stop.

There's something exceedingly depressing about the whole thing. Summer school is an aberration. If God had meant for kids to go to school in the summer, He'd have at least air-conditioned the buildings. As it is it's like being sentenced to a term in hell merely because you thought you knew more algebra than you really did. It's an excessive punishment, to say the least, and may even be unconstitutional.

Summer school is a place for losers, the guys who couldn't deal with "regular" school and end up going to school in July as a result. Visit any average summer school class and you'll find the place is full of hooky players and jocks and bikers and dropouts and similar riffraff. Needless to say, these are the very people you'd most like to avoid, and one way to do that is to stay the hell out of summer school.

With these kinds of "students" in attendance you can imagine how thrilled most teachers are about teaching summer school. Only extreme poverty will motivate a teacher to do so. They regard it as a trial and an ultimate sham. If the kids show up and can drag themselves through the interminable ninety-minute long classes in eighty-five degree heat, they're automatically entitled to a passing grade. Any "work" that goes on is incidental and totally unexpected. Everybody just wants it over with.

I should mention that there are a lot of science-club types in summer school, too. These people actually like it; they don't know anything about playing baseball or hanging out on the corner or getting laid; in brief, they're losers in their own right.

Since these are some more of the people you'd most like to avoid, and since the whole idea of going to school in the summer time is repugnant to Christians everywhere, you should refuse to have anything to do with it.

This book is dedicated to keeping you out of such places. If you learn its lessons well, you'll never have to serve time in a summer school.

## Chapter Fourteen

### Sex Education

Most modern high schools offer a course in sex education, but don't let that fool you. You won't learn much about sex because your teachers are too hung up on it themselves to tell you the truth. The subject embarrasses them and, besides, the real purpose behind these courses is to fill you with alarmist bullshit and misinformation so you won't want to get laid at all.

Take the matter of venereal disease, for example. Instead of telling you the truth about clap and syphilis, that they're thoroughly understood diseases easily treated and cured with modern medicine, they refuse to discuss them at all and insinuate only that your pecker will rot and fall off if you screw around. It's the old army training film dodge: scare the hell out of them and they won't ever want to get laid again.

This AIDS stuff is another matter because it's for real and can fix your wagon pretty good if you don't watch out. The solution to this problem is to practice so-called safe sex and that merely means to use condoms. The condom serves the double purpose of preventing disease and also keeping you girls the hell out of the maternity ward.

Sex-ed classes make it obvious that the authorities don't really want you to learn anything meaningful about sex because the teacher assigned to teach them is usually an old bat who hasn't had a single sex-related thought in years—if ever. She knows almost nothing about real sex, at least not from personal experience. The last hand she felt on her knee probably belonged to a four-foot-high Boy Scout who was stopping her from crossing the street before the light turned green.

The truth is this is one of the few classes where you'll know more about the subject than the teacher does. She'll have to remember all the way back to World War II to recall her last sexual encounter while most of her students will only have to remember as far back as last night. Still, she's confident she's fully qualified to teach sex education to all but the most sexually sophisticated—the kids in her class.

A maxim: the people in charge always feel that half-truths are good enough for peons. It's true everywhere. The President only tells us (political peons) what he wants us to know just as your school principal only tells his teachers (academic peons) what he wants them to know. A chief reason for the universality of this phenomenon lies in the fact that an enlightened peasantry is dangerous and a threat to those in charge.

Look how they teach birth control. They'll talk about it but you'll never see the teacher demonstrate the correct way (usually in great haste) to put a condom on. You just won't ever see such a thing. You won't even see a real rubber, not even one wrapped in tinfoil.

If you persist in asking direct questions about rubbers, you'll be sent down for a good caning for disturbing the class or something. They simply won't tolerate any dirty talk about sex and any of the specific details surrounding it.

Heaven forbid that the teacher should ever mention abortion as a possible solution for the teenage girl who finds herself with child! Anti-choice types would swarm all over the place carrying signs and glass jars filled with fetuses and beating the crap out of any rational person who got in their way.

The principal would panic and call the teacher in for a "conference" where she'd be told to shut the hell up or else, federal funding would be cut off, and the pope would interdict the entire neighborhood and we'd all be denied Christian burial.

In other words, if you girls are going to get any information on abortion, you'll have to get it on your own; it's a cinch you'll never find it in the average high school sex-ed class.

Nor will you ever see the teacher hold a diaphragm up and explain its parts and how it works and where to get one and so on. No one will ever show you how to use the various creams, jellies, foams, and sprays available, either. No one will demonstrate the right way to douche, or hold one up for inspection. As a matter of fact, nobody will even talk about any of this stuff in your sex-ed class.

I might add as an aside here that there is some

hope for a more enlightened attitude about all this on the horizon. A few high schools are planning to sponsor real birth control clinics even as I write this, places where actual condoms are available along with real information on the whole business of birth control. It's also true that people are raising hell about it, too. As for me, I'll believe it when I see it.

Well, what do you get in a sex-ed class then? You get a lot of bullshit that's been approved for your consumption by a committee of local numbskulls and half-wits, that's what you get. A committee of sexually confused and hung-up old geezers sits around in a conference room and decides what you should or should not be told about getting laid.

They'll give you textbooks with silhouette drawings of girls' boobs and guys' dongs and some color pictures of a lot of internal organs made to look as revolting as possible so you won't want anything to do with them. You'll get a lot of talk about sperm and eggs and nothing about people actually getting laid. After a while you'll begin to wonder if the whole thing is a hoax and we're all products of immaculate conceptions.

You'll also get movies. Not good movies such as you see on TV (especially cable) or the ones playing at your local theatre. There won't be any bare boobs and full-frontal nudity and heaving bodies and anguished cries and wild contortions in sex-ed movies.

You'll get boring movies carefully designed to prevent impure thoughts or provide any real information about sex. You certainly won't see anything that might hold your attention even as it informs you such as a good porno flick would. You'll have to see those at home on your DVD—when your hypocritical parents who designed the sex-ed course aren't watching them, that is.

In other words, you get a lot of crap that wouldn't enlighten your average ten-year-old as far as any understanding of sex is concerned. You'll come out as ignorant as when you entered and the authorities will feel they've done everything possible to ensure you a normal, well-adjusted and enjoyable sex life, something they've probably never had for themselves. Don't forget, they took sex-ed courses in high school, too.

The proof that these courses are a joke is evident in the number of teenage girls turning up pregnant all over the place these days. They're a common sight in every school, especially in the larger cities. And not only are pregnant girls a common sight in our schools, but they also stay until the very last minute. I always made it a practice to keep lots of hot water and torn sheets on hand just in case one of them stayed a minute too long.

If high school sex-ed courses are to mean anything, they need to get down to basics and call a spade a spade. Tell the kids the truth without knuckling under to the whims of every two-bit pressure group out there striving mightily to keep them ignorant and "pure" for one asinine reason or another.

If these courses do nothing more, they should give teenagers a good no-holds-barred lesson on the very latest birth control techniques so fewer thirteen- and fourteen-year-old girls will end up pregnant and having babies when they should be trying out for the cheerleader squad and planning for the upcoming prom.

Make sex-ed courses like other academic courses. Have regular lessons, assign homework. Every kid should pick a partner and engage in creative sexual stuff for at least thirty minutes every night. Term papers with footnotes should be required—if any feet were used. Have a final exam that includes a show and tell section. The teacher could have the kids grade each other on a scale of one-to-ten.

Of course, another grading system may have to be devised if the kids scoring tens become so popular with their peers that they find themselves tied up on perpetual dates and falling behind in their classes.

In other words, make sex as real in the classroom as it is in the kids' living rooms and back seats, and give them useful advice on how to deal with it as responsible adults—like you.

Frankly, I don't see any of this happening anytime soon as ignorance and foolishness are too deeply embedded in the average dude's mind out there. This means you guys are on your own. It's your life we're talking about here. Take charge of your own destiny, find out what it's all about before launching yourself on a life of debauchery and sin and you'll enjoy it lot more in the long run.

## Chapter Fifteen

### Homework

Most teenagers regard homework as a pain in the neck—or sometimes a little lower in the anatomy—but its an inevitable part of high school life in all corners of the Earth and must be dealt with. Teachers feel obligated to assign the stuff; in fact, a lot of them take a perverse delight in loading everybody up with stacks of meaningless bullshit to do over the weekend so they won't get into any trouble, i.e., have any fun.

I mean, it goes without saying that three or four hours of homework every night can interfere with more important things like talking on the phone, text messaging, making out, drinking beer, and carousing generally. The question is, then, how can today's high school student deal with homework and still be a survivor?

Fortunately, there are things you can do, but some of them do have drawbacks.

**(A) The Brainy Boy-Girlfriend Ploy**

This one is a classic device known throughout Christendom because it works. All you do is find a class brain of the appropriate (opposite, usually) sex and con them into doing your homework for you. It's easy to do too because most class brains are masochists who love doing homework and otherwise abusing themselves.

However, this is one of those schemes with a drawback to it. Since these smart people aren't stupid they'll want payment for their work, usually in the form of personal attention (sometimes even intimate attention) and that presents a major problem. These guys are the same ones who wear thick glasses, sport braces, and eat garlic sandwiches for lunch. Any red-blooded American high-school student would rather flunk than get within a rod of such people so there's not much hope in this plan. Maybe if they gave up the garlic sandwiches...

**(B) The Team Effort Approach**

With this method you round up six or seven friends and pool your homework. One person does the English, another the math, somebody else does the science, and you meet by the flagpole and swap assignments before first-hour class the next day. Using the Team Effort Approach you can do three hours' worth of homework in thirty minutes and have lots of time left to get out of the house and muck about with the girl who sits across from you in study hall.

One obvious drawback here, of course, is that if you always do the English homework assignments and nothing more you'll remain totally ignorant of everything else in the curriculum and be forced to go through life an ignoramus—but what the hell.

**(C) The Always Hand Something In Ploy**

When an assignment is due and you haven't even started the damn thing, sit down and copy several pages from a book—any book—in scrawled handwriting and hand it in. You never know, lots of times teachers don't read the stuff anyway and give credit to anyone who turns in a paper. Besides, if the handwriting is bad enough most teachers would rather give you the benefit of the doubt than try to read it.

Incidentally, you'd be surprised how often this scam works in the average high school these days, but even if it doesn't what have you got to lose? If you don't turn something in you get an F, and if the old biddy spots your phony homework you get the same F without further penalty. As I said, what have you got to lose?

And there you have the cardinal rule in these matters: always hand something in!

Nothing infuriates a teacher more than to scan the record book and see a whole lot of blank squares following your name. Blank squares tell the teacher you didn't care enough to even try, and if you don't give a damn whether you pass or fail, why should she care?

I always took special pleasure in recording an F for the kid who never did any work. It's a prime example of the old saw about the best laughing being done by the guy who laughs last. After a kid had badgered and irritated me for an entire semester and enjoyed many a hearty laugh at my expense, I'd grin like the Cheshire cat as I savaged his GPA.

On the other hand, even turning in half the required homework can earn you a 50% grade and a string of 50s looks a lot better than all those condemnatory blanks. So remember, always hand something in. After all, a slim chance is better than none.

**(D) Try Lying**

Another popular approach is just to lie about the whole thing. Tell the teacher you turned the assignment in and she must have lost it. Stick to your story no matter what. Be creative. Assume a pious look.

Consider this scene I witnessed at Cody.

Jimmy: (feigns astonishment) "What you mean, you ain't got my homework?"

Miss Shrill: (correcting grammar) "I don't have your homework, Jimmy."

Jimmy: "But I turnt it in, Miss Shrill!" (points) "I put it right there on your desk! I said, 'Here go my homework, Miss Shrill.'"

Miss Shrill: "Jimmy, I do not remember getting homework from you."

At this point Jimmy goes nuts. He runs up and points to the exact spot on the desk where he put the homework, appeals to other kids for support, smites himself on the forehead, and generally acts like an innocent man wrongfully accused.

Jimmy: "But I turnt it in! You was talkin' wif' a girl wearin' a Knicks jacket!" (to nearby kid) "Paco, you seen me give Miss Shrill my homework, ain't you?"

Paco: (pointing) "Yeah, I saw Miss Shrill put it right there, man."

Miss Shrill: (uncertainly) "Are you sure, Jimmy?

I didn't see it with the other papers."

Now you've got her, by God! You detect a slight glimmer of uncertainty in her voice; she's not sure. If you refuse to give in, and make your story good enough, the teacher will begin to doubt the whole damn thing and think maybe you're telling the truth and she really did lose it.

When you see she's beginning to weaken, you boldly demand that she either find your homework assignment or give you an A on it because this was absolutely the best work you'd ever done and it was even typed and everything and you want justice served and so on. While you may not get an A out of it, you'll sure as hell at least get a passing grade for an assignment you didn't even do.

I was going to say you should demand what you've got coming to you but that's a phrase you should never use. God might hear you and actually give you "what you've got coming to you," and you know what that would mean.

A word of caution on this ruse. Remember, you can't use this trick on the teacher more than three or four times before she catches on and starts insisting that you have all future assignments notarized and countersigned by reliable witnesses before you hand them in. I mean, not even the slowest ones can be duped all the time, in spite of what Mr. Lincoln had to say on the subject.

**(E) Excuses**

When all else fails and the homework is due and

you don't have it, you need a good excuse. This calls for a lively imagination and some creative thinking on your part.

Instead of just saying the dog ate it you can embellish this clichéd story by presenting torn, illegible sheets of notebook paper full of teeth marks and drool. Be sure to include lots of drool and the teacher won't even want to touch it, thus assuring that she won't examine it and catch your ass. You can even bring your dog along as further evidence and proof that you actually have a dog.

Another good excuse—especially if you go to school in Detroit—is to claim that some asshole held you up at gunpoint and made off with your homework. Teachers here know the place is full of ignorant assholes who regularly commit armed robbery to get a pair of sneakers off some poor sap's feet so they'll usually buy this story several times a semester.

Girls have some additional excuses they can use which are theirs by virtue of the peculiarities of their sex. So many high school girls are having babies these days that they can always say they don't have their homework because they had to stay up all night taking care of the twins.

One girl at Cody told her teacher she didn't have her homework because she was up all night having a baby and it worked, but another girl lost her case when she told the teacher she didn't have hers because she was up all night making a baby. The teacher gave her an F even though it appeared she'd already had that.

In brief, put some effort into making up good excuses; be creative, original, daring, even. Remember, the more outlandish the story, the more readily they believe it. Show the teacher you really care.

I've known kids who would spend two or three hours coming up with just the right excuse for not having their homework, and all of them went on to the better colleges and universities and became rich, successful, and powerful members of the community by building on the solid foundations they'd established in high school.

Yes, it's true, they could just as easily have done the homework in the same time they spent devising an acceptable scam, but that's a cop out and does nothing to prepare one for modern life which rewards deception and duplicity and double-dealing. Most experts agree that learning to lie and finagle and connive in high school will redound to your lasting benefit ever after in the real world where such traits are highly valued.

## Chapter Sixteen

### The Curriculum — An Overview

It's important that we take a few minutes here to examine some of the courses available to you in high school if you're to make intelligent choices in putting together a schedule. Some courses are easy, some hard. Nerds will be attracted to certain courses that will be anathema to bikers and jocks; others will appeal to girls more than boys and vice-versa, and so on. Make the wrong choices and they'll haunt your ass across continents and into old age.

So let's run over a few of the principal courses and analyze them with an eye to finding out which will best serve your needs.

**(A) Business Courses**

The business department offers typing and bookkeeping and shorthand and similar courses that are boring as dishwater but not without some value. They're especially useful for girls who want to prepare themselves for a lifetime of work as secretaries and general office workers. A good typist can always find work at a salary that beats the minimum wage, and she'll have a chance to snare a husband by moving in on her boss and stealing him away from his lawful wife as bosses are notorious for getting involved romantically with their secretaries. The trouble with this plan, though, is how do you keep his next secretary from stealing him away from you?

Besides just getting a job when you graduate, business courses in high school are a good idea for those who plan to go to college and major in business. Getting a degree in this field is a good move these days since it's become one of the glamour majors. Everybody wants to be another H. Ross Perot or Warren Buffet or insider stock trader on Wall Street and earn millions overnight. This is a good field if you're unscrupulous and greedy; it's a poor one if you're cursed with a conscience and excess (any) moral fiber.

**(B) English**

One of the courses you'll be required to take in every American high school is English. As a matter of fact, even such lackluster schools as those in Detroit demand that each student take a full four years of English to earn a diploma. Of course, we don't actually insist that the kids be able to speak fluent English much less write it properly, but they do have to complete four years of it to graduate.

The real problem with English is that most kids find the stuff astonishingly dull and drier than dust. The eight parts of speech are a total mystery and as arcane to them as the doctrines of the Rosicrucians—and a good deal less interesting.

The intricacies of grammar will anesthetize a teenager faster than a rap on the head with a baseball bat. Reading is something modern kids do only when the TV set breaks down or their iPod explodes on them, and even then they don't choose to read the kind of stuff provided by English teachers.

One way to look at English as a subject in school is to take you to a typical English class at Cody and see how such an operation works in the world of modern high school education.

The bell rings and Miss Shrill stands before her classroom door to greet her students. There are four or five kids already in the room and hundreds milling about in the hall. In another five minutes the late arrivals will be there and Miss Shrill will close the door and begin class.

Once assembled, there are a total of eighteen kids scattered around the room where there should be thirty. A dozen of them have decided they're totally unable to deal with it all and played hooky. Of the eighteen who showed up three are already fast asleep, three more gaze idly through the window, a couple more earnestly take notes and nod as though they know what's going on, and the rest of them wear various expressions ranging from wild disbelief to complete indifference.

Miss Shrill slashes at the board with her chalk, shoots arrows this way and that, underlines this crucial fact and circles that one and scowls the whole time. "...the gerund never follows the verb then," she intones. "Is that clear?" She glares around the room as though daring someone to admit it isn't. Nobody moves.

"Okay," she says, nodding and turning back to the board, "then let's take a look at adverbial phrases and commas used in sequence." Several kids look at each other in complete confusion but the teacher doesn't notice. "Remember the rule that adverbial clauses never appear in prepositional phrases where commas are used in sequence—except, of course, where independent clauses are involved."

Helen Goodbody in the first row shoots a hand skyward.

"Miss Shrill," she asks prettily, "can't adverbial clauses also be used with subjunctives when followed by a pejorative and a linking verb?"

"Of course they can," Miss Shrill says, beaming at the only kid in the room who seems to know what the hell's going on. "That's the exception to the rule and you expressed it nicely."

The teacher turns back to the board and the rest of the kids in the class hurl paper and erasers and other shit at the little bitch for making them all look as bad as they really are.

Miss Shrill launches into still another set of obscure rules with assorted exceptions while the kids flounder in dismay.

"Hey, man," Freddie whispers to another dude wearing a leather cap, "what the fuck she talkin' about?"

"How the hell do I know?" Leather Cap replies, frowning. "We only bin in this class for eight weeks."

"I think it got somethin' to do wif' sentences," the guy in front of Freddie chimes in.

"I don' know nothin' 'bout sentences, but I know it ain't got shit to do wif' me, man."

"...pronouns and adjectives are adjuncts when they're used reflexively." She whirls about and calls on some poor sap in the second row. "Tommy, tell us when reflexive pronouns are used."

Tommy stares wildly around with a look of terror stamped on his face. He looks at his desk, starts turning pages in his book, lifts the book and looks under it as though half expecting to find the answer hiding from him, and generally indicates he hasn't got the faintest idea of what she's talking about.

The teacher sees this at once, of course, but does she spare the poor chump the humiliation of having to squirm under the piercing gaze of his peers as his ignorance is advertised to one and all? Hell, no. She lets him squirm.

Then, after he's squirmed long enough, "Never mind, Tommy, we'll ask someone who hasn't been absent twenty-six times. Sandra?"

Sandra answers hesitantly, "After conjunctions?"

Miss Shrill frowns. "We don't use reflexive pronouns after conjunctions," she says archly.

Jason sees what he thinks is an opportunity and he raises his hand and says, "Before conjunctions?"

Juan sees the teacher start to shake her head and he shouts, "Instead of conjunctions!"

Now the teacher is beside herself. She's worked her fingers to the elbows with these lamebrains and they haven't been able to grasp even the simplest (to her!) concepts regarding the English language. She announces her displeasure to the world.

"Look, I've explained this stuff to you every day for eight weeks and you still haven't caught on! All right, get those notebooks out and open your books to page 126, exercise A. You're going to copy the rules down and memorize them if it takes the rest of the year. Now get busy. List all eight parts of speech, conjugate the verbs through every tense...!"

And so on. The teacher wages a futile fight against ignorance and despair and the kids resist with might and main—and I can safely report that the kids are winning. English just isn't an interesting or worthwhile subject to most teenagers—or senior citizens, either, for that matter. Everybody knows it's the most crucial subject in the curriculum, one that will more directly affect one's life than any other, but it's still boring and dull.

Since you cannot escape from it, though, you have to learn to deal with it. Some ideas presented earlier will help since they work in all classes, and there are specific others that apply to English.

For instance, remember to use your worst handwriting at all times. English teachers have to do a lot of reading while correcting themes, grammar exercises, and so on, and what they hate most is trying to read the chicken scratches most of you call writing. It's a lot easier just to mark it right and move on than it is to spend the night trying to decipher the indecipherable.

And there's the uniquely English exercise of writing book reports, the bane of high school kids everywhere. No kid can possibly expect to go through school without handing in at least fifty or sixty book reports and he needs all his wits to survive such abuse.

One easy way to deal with this problem is just to choose a book you know your teacher would never read in a million years—Motorcycle Gangs of California and Cistern Cleaning for Fun and Profit come to mind—and copy the entire dust jacket in your scrawling handwriting and hand it in. Write in pencil and smudge it a bit. Scratch yourself vigorously as you give it to her. Most teachers would rather give you credit than touch such a paper.

Another approved method, of course, is the old standby of paying a friend who knows how to read to write a book report for you. Or buy an old one from last semester. Or, if you're really a venturesome sort of person, try reading a book and doing your own report. You may surprise yourself, especially if you choose the right book.

Still another method, for those who can actually read a little, is to use Cliff's Notes. Even such a mighty tome as War and Peace is reduced to a page or two and everything is spelled out so even you can grasp it. Include a lot of literary phrases like foreshadowing, conflict, and alliteration, and a passing grade is as good as yours.

(You might make a report on this book because you can bet your ass the teacher hasn't read it—but I won't be responsible for your grade.)

**(C) Home Economics**

You learn to make chocolate pudding here. The instant kind. It's also a good class for boys because there are a lot of girls in it. Best of all, it's an easy A and will do wonders for your GPA. I recommend everyone take a home ec class. In fact, major in the stuff if that's possible.

**(D) Mathematics**

If you like pocket calculators, think engineering would be a great career, and have a poster of Einstein on your bedroom wall, you should take a lot of math courses. Begin with algebra and if that doesn't paralyze your brain altogether go on to geometry and physics and calculus and trigonometry until you learn enough to earn a gold-plated pocket protector for all your pens. You'll also need close-cropped hair and glasses and a lot of polyester shirts.

If you don't want to be an engineer or some kind of molecular scientist, skip math. Studies prove people who don't use math in their work after graduating from school forget the stuff entirely within six months. What's the point of all that work for something you won't remember by the time the ink dries on your diploma?

Besides, math is a bitch to learn. It's got all these esoteric symbols and complicated formulas and it's nearly impossible to fake an answer on a test. I mean, if they give you a formula a foot-and-half-long and ask you what the hell it all means, there's only one answer you can put at the end of it.

You can't write out a page of bullshit explaining what you think it may mean; you either put down the right answer, or the damn thing is wrong, period. How the hell can they expect you to pass a class like that?

What about your college plans? Won't your failure to take lots of math hurt you there? No, not if you major in fields where math isn't needed. English and journalism and art and hundreds of other majors have almost no math requirements at all or, at most, a course in simple arithmetic to be sure you at least know how to add.

So easy does it on those math courses.

**(E) Foreign Languages**

Who needs them? Look, if those foreigners want to talk to you, let them learn English, by God. After all, aren't we the high muck-a-mucks on this tired old globe? Isn't English the most widely spoken language of them all? When the Roman Empire was at the height of its power, did the Romans go around learning how to speak Greek and Arabic? Hell, no. They made everybody else learn Latin and that's as it should be.

Don't worry about it. If you go abroad and find yourself surrounded by foreigners, just speak up in a loud voice and let them know you want somebody who can speak English and you want them quick. Let them know you're an American and not someone to be trifled with, by God. And if they give you a hard time, just tell them you'll take your American money elsewhere and watch them shape up in a hurry.

Besides, learning a foreign language isn't easy. You sign up for French and there's a good chance your GPA will take it in the neck. French will require endless hours of conjugating verbs and you know how dull that is even when the verbs are in a language you're familiar with.

But if you do decide to take a foreign language, make it Spanish. At the rate things are going in this country today, it's just a matter of time until we're all speaking Spanish, anyway, so you may as well get a head start on them.

All that said it's pretty cool to be bi-lingual. All you Hispanic and Asian guys out there are a cut above the rest of us in that regard. The next time some asshole puts you down, give him a good tongue lashing in Spanish or Vietnamese and confuse his ass.

**(F) Science**

Science includes all those really hard courses like chemistry and biology and zoology and you don't need them if you plan to grow up to be a regular American. The average guy in the street wouldn't know a chemical formula from an amoebae and he's none the worse for it. Doctors and research chemists and dentists need these courses so take them if you plan these careers, otherwise give them a miss.

**(G) Shop**

Shop classes are great for building those GPAs because of the easy grades you can earn in them, but you pay a price in other ways. For one thing there's the physical danger involved, especially in wood shop.

Did you ever take a close look at the average wood shop teacher? These guys are always short three or four fingers, aren't they? Apparently, none of them knows anything about safety and power saws.

It's true. You start a piece of wood through that baby and you get distracted for a minute and the next thing you know you've sliced through the wood, four or five fingers, and half a thumb. People start calling you Stubby and the only career you're fit for is wood shop teacher because you have so much in common with the rest of them.

What's more, shop is dirty. Even if you do manage to keep all your fingers, you still go through life with eternally dirty fingernails and hands that require Lava soap and lye to cut the grease and grime. If you have an aversion to dirt you might find shop classes a little rough even if they do raise your GPA.

Of course, bikers and jocks and apprentice chop shop operators don't care anything about a little dirt and that's an additional drawback to shop classes because these are the kind of people you'll find there. Shop is a major for these guys; they make it a career.

If you sign up for one of these classes you'll likely have to share a workbench with a guy wearing a leather jacket and the Saturn-like rings of unsavory air that accompany the unwashed everywhere. Still, it may be worth it if you're desperate enough—and most of you are.

In addition to the above there are a lot of miscellaneous courses such as art and music and drama that can usually be counted on for a fairly easy grade and don't require any more work than you're willing to do, which is to say, none. These courses usually attract girls so that's another plus—unless you're a girl, of course. They also look good on your transcript because it gives the illusion that you're well rounded and that appeals to college admissions types in our better universities.

Remember, it's important that you think the matter through before choosing a curriculum. Make the wrong choices and you'll end up with the wrong friends and headed for the wrong career. Grandpa Ganja knows this from personal experience, unfortunately.

We'll take a closer look at possible career choices later on and that will help start you in the right direction.

## Chapter Seventeen

### Weapons in Schools

This section is aimed at high school kids who live in places known for violence and unbridled ignorance, places like Detroit and New York and Chicago and L.A. and other larger cities. If you live in a town where everybody isn't busy killing or maiming his neighbor, you can safely skip this chapter.

Okay, so how do you know if there are weapons in your school? How can you find such a thing out? Well, it happens I'm an expert on such matters and I've come up with a sure-fire system for determining which schools are safe and which are armed camps.

One way to tell if there are guns and knives in your school is to look for any kids with bullet holes and stab wounds in them. You might find them in the john or lying in a stairwell or staggering into your English class and bleeding all over the place. If you see much of this sort of thing, chances are you go to school in Detroit.

Another thing to look for is a suspicious bulge in kids' clothes. If you see a bulge in a kid's pants he just might have a gun in there. (Remember Mae West, though. It may be a gun or he may just be glad to see you.) In fact, with the average teenager's propensity for having perpetual erections there's a good chance you'll reach in for a gun and come out with some guy's dork, for God's sake.

    You can also listen for gunshots going off around the school. That's a dead giveaway that there are guns in the vicinity but learn to tell the difference between gunshots and backfires so you won't be fooled and fly into unnecessary panics every few minutes. One thing to remember is that backfires don't ricochet or make holes in nearby windows and walls. Offhand, I'd say if you've got more than four or five gunshots a day on your campus you've got a problem and should act accordingly.

    Bullet holes are another good way to tell how many guns there are in a given school. You can figure a ratio of one gun for every four holes. If the walls of your school look like a gang of Taliban cutthroats just passed through you can assume there are guns around somewhere.

    And spent shell cases are another tip-off. If the campus looks like a firing range for the National Rifle Association, there are guns in the vicinity.

    Weapons will reveal themselves in subtle ways, too, if the observer is alert. If the teacher asks for a knife to cut some twine or something and eight or ten guys whip out foot-long switchblades, you'll know all is not right around you.

    You can keep track of crime in your schools by reading the local newspapers. Reporters love stories of shootings and stabbings and they gleefully write elaborate accounts of each and every one that takes place in their corner of the state. It's the stuff that sells newspapers. All big city newspapers have most of their staff assigned to the crime beat so it's not likely they'll miss any shooting at the local high school.

So read the papers in your town. Keep posted. It's a good idea to keep your finger on your pulse to get the sense of things—and make sure the damn thing is still working.

Okay, then. You watch for the signs listed above and you find out a lot of people at your school are armed to the teeth. What do you do about it? You refer school officials to the suggestions below; that's what you do. Each of these schemes has been tried without effect in the Detroit schools, but at least they make it seem like you care.

First, insist that the school board hire some cops for each high school. Get big ones, ugly ones, if possible. Have them patrol the halls and campus with orders to arrest every troublemaker they see. Keep some trucks nearby to haul the troublemakers away.

For a school project, you can sell bulletproof vests to your classmates and make handsome profits while providing a useful service. The damn things sell like hotcakes in Detroit schools; even the teachers wear them. One year the senior class sold enough bulletproof vests to send the whole class to Rio on their senior trip.

Metal detectors are still another way to fight weapons in our schools. We've been using them in Detroit for several years now and they're an unqualified success. You get one of those units like they use at the airports and set the thing up in the gym unannounced.

When the kids show up in the morning you route them through the gym where somebody goes over them with this wand gadget. If the alarm sounds the kid is hauled away and strip-searched for weapons. We find dozens of guns and knives every time we use this machine, but we don't actually find them with the machine itself. We find them on the floor where the kids drop them before they get to the machine.

And as we've seen you need to keep a close eye on the honor roll kid who gets all A's; the asshole probably has a gun in every pocket and is just waiting for a chance to decimate his English class.

Institute a policy popular in the saloons of the Wild West: make everybody check his guns at the door on the way in and pick them up as he leaves. Of course, this scheme will only work if the kids are willing to cooperate and voluntarily agree to disarm themselves, a not very promising prospect.

Urge the school board to buy some Dobermans trained to sniff out guns and knives and turn them loose in the place. Even if they never actually find any weapons, they'll intimidate the hell out of everybody and that's just as good.

One final bit of advice: if school boards are serious about driving the weapons out of your school they should show they mean business by coming down hard on people they catch carrying them. The kind of guy who brings his .45 to school is likely to be an ignorant asshole with a short attention span; you need to get his attention before you can make him understand what's going on, and one way to do that is to punish his ass so he won't soon forget it.

Detroit schools have adopted a new get-tough policy in recent years. If they catch a kid with a gun in a Detroit school these days he's immediately suspended for up to three days while a hearing is arranged—and to give him time to hire a lawyer. If he's found guilty he's transferred forthwith to another school as much as a mile away from his present one. And if he actually shoots somebody they show him they mean business and make him go to night school, by God!

I've heard of a few cases where an armed student was kicked completely out of the school system, but I can't vouch for the truth of these rumors. Everyone realizes that total expulsion from school is pretty heavy stuff and may not even be constitutional the way things are going nowadays.

Anyway, give some of these schemes a try if kids plague your school with weapons. They won't work, of course, but you'll feel you're accomplishing something even though you aren't.

In the end you have to learn to live with the reality of things, i.e., how to survive. Always keep your back to the wall and never sit near windows. Avoid crowds. Wear your bulletproof vest at all times. Never give a sucker an even break and stay away from those honor students.

Remember, in order to survive high school it's necessary that you still be alive at graduation.

## Chapter Eighteen

### Substitute Teachers

Let's face it, a sub in the class means a day off. In fact, a lot of kids literally take off as soon as they see there's a sub because they know they can lie and swear they were there when the regular teacher returns. Regular teachers easily buy this story since most of them regard the average sub as a gross incompetent who is so jaded by constant exposure to terror and anxiety that she no longer gives a damn and makes no effort to do things right.

And even the kids who do go to class have the day off because they know the sub isn't really in charge of things. For instance, if you screw around with your regular teacher she'll haul your ass off to the office or fetch a counselor or even call your parents and raise hell, but the sub can't really do any of these things.

Half the time the sub doesn't even know anybody's name because the regular teacher didn't leave seating charts. And if the sub complains too much to the office or counselors she quickly gets a reputation as someone who can't handle things on her own and the school officials will ask that she not be sent back as a sub in that school.

This isn't true in Detroit, of course, where there's usually such a shortage of subs that any living creature will be welcomed with open arms. I know whereof I speak because when no sub was available for an absent teacher in my department, guess who had to cover that class? I'd settle for a stick figure rather than have to man the trenches myself.

It's not really necessary to bother doing the work assigned to you by a sub since most teachers just leave busy work for the sub, anyway. It's often not even checked; in fact, it's often not even turned in by the sub because she manages to lose your papers by the end of the day.

Some kids have been known to cause such losses by stealing the papers from her desk on the way out and tossing them in the nearest wastebasket. The sub doesn't mind, as she knows no one expects much of her anyway, and the teacher doesn't care because it means she won't have to bother checking the papers.

If the sub is an experienced old-timer, she'll probably show up with the morning paper tucked under her arm. She'll write the assignment on the board, pass out some writing paper, and spend the day reading her newspaper while you sail paper airplanes, throw lighted matches around, and socialize with your friends. If the principal passes by he'll pretend not to notice as long as the noise level isn't so high as to bring complaints from nearby teachers who are trying to do some work.

Not every sub falls in the incompetent category, though. Some of them are tough old birds that come in and kick ass and let you know right from the start they won't tolerate any crap. You can always tell these types because they come in scowling and grab the first troublemaker by the throat that shows his true colors and proceed to straighten his ass out on the spot.

These old biddies will march the whole class down to the principal's office and demand that the old fraud do his job and enforce some discipline for a change. I've even seen some who went to the trouble of getting a kid's real name and phone number and calling his parents to report his ass for unseemly behavior.

If one of these guys shows up you'd be well advised to save the paper airplanes and lighted matches for the next incompetent sub you meet and leave this one the hell alone. It might even be a good idea to do some work in the class because she won't lose the papers. Some of them go so far as to actually check the papers themselves so all the regular teacher has to do is record the grades, and few regular teachers are so lazy they won't do that.

Finally, let's take a minute here to plead for compassion in at least some cases. A lot of these subs are emotionally unstable people who subsist on a diet of tranquilizers and nerve tonic. Maybe they're former regular teachers who came apart and had to give it up, or they may be old widows who've had to go back to work late in life and are unable to come to terms with the modern teenager but, whatever the case, they usually need the money or they wouldn't subject themselves to such humiliation and terror.

So go easy on them if you see they're especially

vulnerable. I know the temptation to run amuck is a powerful one, but give them a break. It's a sad sight to reduce an old lady to tears or cause some dude to snap and start throwing furniture and have an EMS crew cart him away in one of those jackets with the wrap-around sleeves.

After all, it's the Christian thing to do, isn't it?

## Chapter Nineteen

### Prayer in School

As you know, it's strictly illegal to pray in a public school in this country. Anyone caught talking to any god real or imagined is subject to an indefinite term in prison and/or a huge fine. I'm not sure but I think this proscription also applies to consorting with devils, sorcerers, voodooists, imps, succubi, and assorted otherworld beings. If you know of anyone who has dealings with deities/devils in school, report him at once to the authorities and you may be eligible for a substantial reward.

No prayers allowed means when you walk into your English class and the teacher hands you a test you'd completely forgotten was due that day you'd not be allowed to call on God for help. This isn't exactly the hardship it at first appears to be since there's no recorded instance of God actually helping a student in such a case, but there's at least a psychological loss in knowing you'll have to rely entirely on your own resources and no "miracle" will come to your aid.

In other words, it won't help to ask for an earthquake or a sudden power failure or a torrential flood to appear and cause school to be dismissed even if they do allow you to pray for such relief. Still, in the old days you could at least ask for divine intervention even if there wasn't much hope of getting it. Now you know you're screwed, period. God won't help because you aren't allowed to ask Him for any help.

If the kids can't pray in school, what about the teachers? Many a time I've personally heard teachers at Cody say things like, "May God help us!" and "For God's sake, don't shoot!" and "Thank God he missed me!" and so on. Are such appeals to a divine being legal? Are these teachers mixing religion and government in violation of the U.S. Constitution?

Sure, they are, and you would too if you were gazing down the barrel of some sap's revolver and looking for any possible source of assistance no matter how remote. I say we have to allow prayer in the public schools as long as we allow thugs and felons to attend them. Who the hell can we turn to if we can't call on the delusion of our choice in times of such stress?

We all know we can't rely on the authorities to save us from these assholes; the teachers and administrators are as afraid of these guys as the kids are and the cops are too busy busting harmless pot tokers and dunking donuts to stop the bastards. Who's left except God, for Christ's sake?

Well, I guess the answer is to pray when you really have to but just be sure nobody hears you do it. If the teacher is looking around the room for someone to call on and humiliate before the entire class and you lost your textbook three weeks ago and don't even know what chapter they're on, don't panic and shout, "Oh, God, don't let her pick me!"

You'd no sooner get the words out of your

mouth than the prayer police would sweep in and arrest your ass for praying in a public school and haul you off for a spiritual delousing and thorough purging by flagellation or worse.

The thing is to keep your cool and bob and weave behind the guy in front of you and silently ask God to earthquake the place to the ground before she spots your ass. If you're careful not to let anyone see your lips move, you could sneak in a short prayer and no one would be the wiser.

And who knows? It's worth the risk. You might be the very first guy it ever worked for. If it does let Grandpa Ganja know at once, as I'll have some fences that need mending.

## Chapter Twenty

### Principals

The principal intimidates everybody. The kids fear the old geezer because he's the final arbiter, the dude who holds expulsion hearings and recommends long prison sentences, and the teachers are afraid of him for the same reasons. Nothing produces greater anxiety in teachers and kids alike than the chilling words, "The principal wants to see you."

Well, the truth is the principal is usually just as intimidated by staff and kids as they are by him because he's worried about how his own bosses will perceive him. If he screws up he'll have the superintendent and the whole school board on his ass and he knows it. That's why the spineless fraud will back and fill and kowtow to every pressure group and irate parent who confronts him.

Consider: the principal gets to be principal in the first place by politicking, that is, by bobbing and weaving and obsequiousness and making the right friends and so on. He doesn't get the job because he's the smartest or best teacher or even best potential administrator; he gets the job because he wheels and deals the right people.

This means that he will automatically lack backbone since people with lots of backbone find it hard to tolerate the half-wits and nincompoops one must befriend if one is to secure their favor. As a result you end up with a gutless dude who puts up a bold front with underlings and bows and scrapes whenever anyone appears on the scene who might cause trouble for him. In other words, you get a politician, a humbug, a lickspittle, a sycophant, or something similar; what you don't get is a fearless, innovative, imaginative leader who is able to run the place with any kind of efficiency.

Since we know he's a humbug it's a good idea to out humbug him. When you fill out your records on arriving at high school claim your father is an important judge or chief of surgery somewhere (say he's your stepdad to explain dissimilar names) or a high muck-a-muck of some other kind and that he has lots of clout.

The principal will find this out when he goes over your records preparing his case against you and I guarantee he'll proceed with caution. No sane principal is going to cause any grief for an important judge or community leader, not if it means potential trouble for him.

Didn't I tell you they're spineless?

Insist that you be allowed to tape record all meetings that take place in his office. Explain that your lawyer has instructed you to do so for possible use in later lawsuits. To provide a nice touch, stop by a lawyer's office and filch some of his cards and leave one with the principal after your first meeting. Don't worry, he won't call, and even if he does just tell him that you've dismissed that lawyer and have another one who will contact him in the morning. Remember the name of the game is bullshit.

Some principals never leave their offices; you never see them in the halls or on the campus. They sneak in early in the morning and don't come out until everybody's gone at night. They rule by memo and the school PA system. They interrupt classes every fifteen minutes with some trivial announcement just to let you know they're still around, but you still don't see them. These kinds are usually afraid of their own shadows and hide out so as to avoid potential trouble.

In Detroit, of course, the principal often hides in his office because he's afraid somebody will kill him if he shows his face anywhere. Sometimes even this tactic won't save his ass, though. I remember in one school where I taught some kids threw big chunks of concrete through the window in the principal's office and the next day his desk was moved over to the far wall and a steel plate was nailed over the window. Since he refused to come out, they went in after his ass.

Other types are sneaky bastards who prowl around the school spying on everybody. They pop in and out of the johns, tiptoe up and peer in classrooms, drop in on the teachers' lounge to see if they can catch somebody zonked out in the Lazy Boy lounger, patrol the parking lots looking for dopers, and generally make a nuisance of themselves. These guys love to "write people up." They're forever putting derogatory letters in teachers' files and ordering suspension hearings for students caught in their dragnets.

If your principal is one of these types, you've got a problem. The best thing you can do with these guys is to stay the hell out of their way. You can, if the need for action arises, also wage a guerrilla war.

Sign his name to love notes written to the drama teacher and leave them in conspicuous places. Make up phony phone messages to him from the substance abuse control center advising him of the next meeting and leave them around the office. Send anonymous letters to the school board asking that he be made to explain the peepholes in the girls' locker room wall, and so on. You can have the bastard on the defensive in no time and keep him so busy trying to clear his name that he won't have time for you.

The main thing to remember about principals is that they're mostly nondescript dudes who are very insecure and feel constantly threatened by everybody. The best defense against them is a good offense. If they monkey around with you, undermine their ass. Be creative. Above all, don't let them intimidate you.

## Chapter Twenty-One

### Class Conduct

It's important that you learn the proper etiquette required in all classrooms everywhere if you're going to survive high school. There are basic rules that every successful survivor has practiced for years, and it's up to you to familiarize yourself with them.

Take sleeping in class. Everybody does it. Most high school classes are so dull they'd cure a severe case of insomnia in ten minutes flat. Even the teachers fall asleep. If you don't believe me, watch them. When she sits in the back of the room while the kids give their boring oral reports, glance back there and see if the old biddy's eyelids don't flutter and droop and her head start down and jerk back up with a violent jolt every thirty seconds or so. She's just as bored as you are.

Okay, if you're going to sleep just remember the universally accepted excuse.

Teacher: "Johnny, wake up!"

Johnny: (jolting awake) "I wasn't asleep; I was just resting my eyes."

Of course everybody knows you were out like a light, but they also know they do it all the time themselves so they're reluctant to push the matter since they'll be using the same excuse the next time they're caught.

Be crafty about it if you're going to sleep. Take

your pen in hand and assume a writing pose with your head down. If you hold that pose, the teacher will think you're taking notes and you can get in a quick nap before anyone's the wiser.

You can also hold a pen in your hand and when you fall asleep the pen will drop on the floor and wake you up. A lot of people use this trick; sometimes you can hear pens dropping all over the place and watch heads snapping up like a lot of jacks in the box.

Some really skillful sleepers can look the teacher straight in the eye and just let their eyes glaze over while remaining wide open. They fall dead asleep and never close their eyes. These people are to be envied, as it's a natural talent, one that can't be learned.

We all know how slowly time goes in school, still it's a mistake to look at your watch and suddenly sit bolt upright and stare at it in disbelief, shake it and hold it to your ear, and generally indicate that your watch must have stopped as there couldn't possibly be nearly an hour to go before the bell, etc.

On seeing this display the teacher will get the idea that you find her class less than stimulating and mark you down as a loser. You can avoid this by refusing to look at your watch no matter how many hours you think have gone by. Just wait for the bell. It only seems like it will never ring.

Don't pass notes for other people in class. It never fails, the guy behind you asks you to pass a note to the dude up front and whom does the teacher catch right in the act? Damn right. And isn't the note unsigned and doesn't it always say something like the teacher's a dope and she has a neck like a turkey and so on? And does she believe you when you insist it isn't your note? Are you kidding?

So don't pass notes unless they're your own. And if you must pass notes, be sure they're not incriminating ones. Don't tell Sally how you hope her parents go out this weekend so you can use their bedroom again. The teacher will intercept this kind of note every time and you'll have to do some pretty tall explaining to Sally's old man and all because you put it in writing.

Okay, now for a look at a special problem for you guys. You know the one I mean, we touched on it earlier. You're sitting in class bored to death as usual when Peggy the Tart sitting across from you and wearing a skirt that reaches all the way down almost to the middle of her thigh begins to get careless with said skirt. The next thing you know the little chippy is providing you with sights wondrous to behold and you end up with a massive erection.

That's right, you know what happens next. The teacher calls on you to come up to the front of the room and recite. The old bat won't call on you all semester until Peggy has done her stuff and then she gets you every time. You know if you start for the front of the room and trip you'll pole vault clear across the teacher's desk. What to do?

Your first thought is to stall for time. If you can just gain a minute or two the thing will go away, or at least shrink to the size of a cop's nightstick from its present baseball bat size.

"Leon?" she says.

You reach over and poke the guy next to you.

"Hey, man, she's callin' you."

"She ain't callin' me, man. She's callin you."

"Leon, will you come up here?" the teacher says. "We don't have all day, you know."

"Uh, teacher, could you call on somebody else and get me next time?" you say.

"No, I couldn't. Get up here this very minute, Leon Trotsky!"

Now you're in for it. No more stalling. You've managed to tear your eyes away from Peggy the Tart but everywhere you look you see some beauty leaning over and spilling out of her blouse or your gaze lights on somebody's naked thigh and the Little General is standing at attention like a soldier on parade. You've got to get up.

If you've got a jacket or something you can always grab it and hold it in front of you but you don't have one handy. The only thing left to do is march to the front of the room with your book in hand and stand holding the book in front of your enormous member. Of course, everybody in the room will see at once what's going on, but it's better to hide what you can than stand totally exposed to the world.

Humiliating as this experience is, it may redound to your benefit when some of the girls get a gander at the size of the thing and decide to examine it at greater length and from a closer perspective later on. It may even result in your social life improving immeasurably, but it's still a damned embarrassing moment, isn't it?

Incidentally, a time may come later when you'll sorely miss the good old days when spontaneous erections plagued you in class. Ask any old-timer.

Talking to your friends in class also requires a certain form—unless you go to school in Detroit. In this burg anybody who has anything to say just says it, and usually at the top of his voice.

"Hey, man, how much you want for that weed?"
"Who got a pencil?"
"Here go a pencil. Who got some paper?"
"Hey, motherfucker, you walkin' on my shoes!"
"Teacher, that dude done stole my hat!"

But you can't do this in most real schools. You need to learn to talk out of the side of your mouth, whisper behind a cupped hand, wait for the teacher to turn her back before calling to the guy across the room, and so on.

Remember to bob and weave. Practice saying "Pssst!" If the teacher asks you to stop talking, deny it was you. Learn some Spanish so you can blame it on the Mexican kid. Be creative. If you can't talk or sleep or pass notes or do something the monotony of it all will short out your neurons and turn your brain into mush.

Finally, it's not a good idea to smoke dope before going to class, as the dope tends to make everything exaggerated and all out of proportion. This means if you go to a really boring world history class it'll seem even more boring than it otherwise would and you may suffer side effects such as terminal boredom and the dreaded creeping ennui.

A lot of times the guy who does the number mentioned above with his watch is somebody who just polished off a joint in the parking lot. It seems like he's been sitting in that class for at least six hours or so and he takes a peek at his watch and is appalled to learn he's only been there ten minutes.

Besides, it's tough when the teacher calls on you and you have to try to make some kind of sense lest everybody find out you've blown your mind again. I've seen kids take five minutes just to figure out what the question was and coming up with an acceptable answer was a million-to-one shot.

It's hard to be a survivor when you can't remember what it is you're trying to survive.

## Chapter Twenty-Two

### Hall Passes

Most schools use hall passes in an effort to keep kids out of the halls and in the classrooms where they belong. If you want to go to the john the teacher has to write out a pass indicating where you're going, the time you left her room, the date, your name, and her signature. Some schools also require a cash deposit that is refundable only if and when you return.

Naturally, everybody regards these passes as a nuisance. The teachers hate to write the damn things because it takes so much time and interferes with whatever learning may be going on in the room at the moment. It never fails, somebody wants a pass to the john just at some crucial moment in the lesson; for instance, just when she's finally gotten everybody's attention and is about to actually teach something for a change. By the time she finishes screwing around with the hall pass the class disintegrates into chaos and the magic moment is lost.

Since teachers don't like to write passes they sometimes don't bother and just tell the kid to get to his locker and hurry back. Of course, the principal will be out in the hall every time and he'll drag the kid back to class and demand to know what the hell he was doing out in the hall without a pass, etc. The teacher gets chewed out in front of everybody and she hates hall passes even more—almost as much as she does that asshole principal.

It happens there are ways to get around the hall pass business. One of the easiest scams is to just carry a piece of paper about the size and shape of the regular hall pass in your school. Nine teachers out of ten will not bother challenging a kid who marches boldly down the hall with said paper held conspicuously in his hand.

It's imperative, of course, that you assume an innocent look. If you're skulking along ducking in and out of doorways and peeking around corners, every teacher will know at once you're up to no good and challenge your ass on the spot.

Look them right in the eye as you approach. It's a good tactic to say hello. Show them you're on the up and up, that your conscience is clear. Smile. Even better, as you draw near, offer to show them your pass. Hand it to them before they even ask for it. Say, "Here go my pass, Miss Grinde," and hand it over. There isn't one teacher in a hundred who'd waste her time by actually reading a pass from such a student. Hell, I'd let a kid with balls like that drive off in the principal's car and never give it a thought.

It's all in the wrist, as they say. All style and no substance, that's the American way. Get by on nerve alone, bullshit your way through and enjoy an unlimited future wherever you go. Even if they catch you red-handed with that blank piece of paper everyone will admire your sense of style and audacity and you'll surely get off with no more serious punishment than a warning not to do it again. It's a risk-free dodge we're talking about here.

However, once they've nailed your ass five or six times with the blank paper for a pass scam, they'll begin to feel threatened and insist on more serious punishment. That's when you move on to some other scheme.

This one is clever and easy. When you leave the room with a legitimate pass, don't hand it in when you come back unless the teacher asks for it. You'll easily be able to alter the date, time, etc., and use the damn thing the next time you want to sneak out for a quick smoke or a cold one.

You can also steal a pad of passes from the teacher's desk and forge one as needed. A lot of teachers keep rubber stamps in their desks with their signatures on them and you can stamp a whole pad ahead of time and have authentic looking passes for any and all events.

Some of the slower teachers even stamp a whole pad of blank passes and leave them lying around loose in their desks, but it's not very sporting to take advantage of these guys as they're obviously not your mental equals.

A caveat, though: they'll get a helluva lot angrier with your ass if they catch you with the signed passes, as this is considered a kind of legal forgery and even a major crime. In fact, if some of the teachers had their way, you'd end up in the big house on this one.

Another device that works pretty well is carrying one of the so-called permanent passes, the kind counselors and others often have for use by their aides, et al. It's usually a wooden pass with a room number or "counseling center" or somebody's name stamped on it.

If they use such passes in your school, get yourself a piece of wood and stamp something on it. Be creative again. Put your own name on it. Or just stamp "office" on the damn thing and head out into the halls safe in the knowledge that almost no one will follow up on its authenticity.

And the beauty of this one is even if you're caught with your homemade pass, what law have you broken? There's a rule against carrying a piece of wood through the halls? Is it your fault people see your piece of wood and assume it's a hall pass? Not in America, it isn't, by God! This is still a democracy and we don't penalize creativity and ingenuity here—and I hope I never see the day when we do.

So, armed with this knowledge, you're ready to wander the halls hither and yon in search of a friendly john or a rendezvous with a friend. Tell them I said it's all right.

## Chapter Twenty-Three

### Dating

Well, the truth is Grandpa Ganja doesn't know very much about dating because it's been fifty-five years since I dated anybody. I'm afraid I can't offer much advice that you'd find useful and you know how I disapprove of bullshit, so I'll make this a short chapter.

A point or two. Don't expect to marry the people you date in high school. It's too soon to hook up with a lifelong partner in your teens, as there are lots of cool people out there you haven't met yet, more mature people better able to make good choices. High school dating is rehearsal time to get ready for the big show later—much later, one would hope.

There are few greater mistakes for teenagers than pregnancy. Don't get pregnant. As for guys, being a dad at eighteen is not a good thing. Think about it.

Treat each other with respect; your dates are people, too.

## Chapter Twenty-Four

### Parent Conferences

Every school principal likes to hold parent conference meetings as a PR tool. It's a way of showing the school is interested in the community and it looks good in reports to the superintendent's office. You will not hold these events in high esteem, though, since they represent a real peril to your own well-being.

You know how they work. Parents are invited to visit the school and confer with your teachers, something that will rarely redound to your benefit. It's bad enough that you have to explain those report cards four or five times a year, but it's even worse when your teachers meet your parents face-to-face and get a chance to tell them the truth about you. After all, how many people can stand having the truth told about them?

There are several things you can do to mitigate the damage done at these conferences and one is to have your parents not show up. The best way to do this is to prevent them from ever hearing about the conference in the first place. You do so by not telling them about it. When notices are given to you to take home, lose yours. Of course, you'll follow the advice given earlier and intercept all mail from the school so if they mail it home your folks will never lay eyes on it.

Everybody at Cody has followed this practice

for years. When we gave them notices to take home the entire campus was littered with the damn things five minutes after school was dismissed. They even threw them away in the halls and on the floor in the room where we handed them out. There probably weren't a dozen kids in the place who took them home and it showed when the conferences were held because we never got more than a handful of parents to show up.

All right, but suppose your parents find out about the conference, anyway? Then what? Well, there are some things you can do. The usual plan calls for your folks to go from room to room meeting your individual teachers. Okay, if you're in your biggest trouble in math you just save math until last. There's a good chance your folks won't get there as they normally have to wait to see each teacher and they'll run out of time.

To slow them up you can direct your parents to a classroom where nine or ten parents are lined up to see the teacher and have them sit there for twenty minutes before suddenly "realizing" that you're in the wrong room. Your old man will be steamed because you're such an idiot but that's better than having him meet Miss Shrill and learn even darker truths.

One device that works is to hire some older people to pose as your parents. Get one of those guys who deliver handbills in the neighborhood or recruit some dude who hangs out in your favorite pool hall and slip him ten bucks. All he has to do is sit there and blink once in a while and maybe throw in a frown at some particularly revealing truth about you and you're home free.

Use some judgment, though. I know a black guy who brought in a Norwegian dude and said he was his old man. Another kid came in with a girl about twenty-two and claimed she was his mother and a girl brought a woman in who was about ninety and said she was her mother. I mean, give the teachers credit for a little intelligence, for Christ's sake. You can't expect to fool people without going to at least a little trouble to do it right.

Other scams that will work in an emergency: have a friend set off a false fire alarm as you're heading toward Miss Shrill's room and they'll have to evacuate the building and waste valuable time. Pretend to have some sort of attack and fall down and writhe all over the place and they'll have to rush you to emergency. Pray (inaudibly) for God to earthquake the place to the ground for you, or try to bribe Miss Shrill the day before, or just take off at a dead run and try to make it to the border.

If all else fails, take your medicine like a man. After all, you screwed up and now's the time to pay the price. Look them straight in the eye and admit you're an asshole—and crawl and whine and beg for a second chance and promise to do better and so on.

It's the only honorable thing to do.

## Chapter Twenty-Five

### Fire Drills

The law requires that every school have a specified number of fire drills each year in order to ensure that everyone knows what to do when some degenerate torches the place. Accordingly, the principal will schedule periodic fire drills to comply with the law and help avoid potential lawsuits.

We don't have any fire drills in Detroit schools because the place catches on fire so often we don't need them; we're already marching out through the actual flames and smoke of real fires every few weeks and don't need the practice.

In fact, we're so inured to fires that we don't usually leave the building during small- to medium-sized infernos if the weather is inclement—which it always is in Motown. Everybody piles up around the exits and waits for the all clear to sound and the firemen get pissed because the kids are blocking the entrances and they can't get in to fight the fire.

Naturally, the principal wants people to get the hell out of the building and not clog up the exits and he hollers at the teachers to get the kids out and the teachers try and fail. We get exchanges like the following.

Teacher: "Hey! Get outside! Don't clog the exits! Get the hell out of the building!"

Student voices: "Fuck you!"

These drills can be a godsend for you. You're sitting in algebra and on the point of being overcome with boredom. You've counted the little holes in the ceiling tiles, stared out of the window, carved your entire name in the desktop, and got a permanent crick in your neck from trying to see up the Peggy the Tart's skirt.

Just when you think you can't stand another minute of it the fire alarm sounds and you're saved. The lesson stops, everybody heads for the door and then outside, people mill around on the grass for a while, and the period ends before you get back in.

Or a fire drill interrupts a world history test that you're in the act of failing and you get to go outside and spend twenty minutes getting answers from somebody who knows what's going on. In such a case a timely fire drill could mean the difference between failing and passing and getting into the right college.

What's more, you can arrange your very own fire drill if you're so inclined. You might even consider it a kind of public service; you want to be sure the school meets its quota for the year and the kids get lots of practice. A quick flip of the lever and you empty the building. What could be easier?

Of course, if you do this too often they'll consider you a menace and set about catching you in the act so they can expel your ass. One way they'll try to catch you is by putting infrared dye on the lever, the kind that shows up purple only under a certain light.

They'll run everybody through those lights and you'll be caught red, er, purple-handed.

Actually, when you stop to think about it, it isn't necessary to run everybody through the lights. They wouldn't start with the honor-roll kids, would they? Or the nerds? Of course not. They'd round up the known troublemakers (you) and start with them and they'd have their man without bothering the other 90% of the student body.

Even so, don't worry about it. Everybody thinks pulling a false fire alarm is a major felony punishable by many years in the big house but the truth is they'll slap your wrist and order you to do a half-hour of community service. It's a small price to pay for getting out of a history final or staving off terminal boredom.

Another ploy involves the ever-popular bomb threat, a gambit that can work as well as the phony fire drill discussed above. All it takes is a phone and a devious mind. It helps if you can lend an air of authenticity to your bomb threat by specifying a particular kind of bomb rather than relying solely on the generic term.

When you call say that you've planted six sticks of grade-A dynamite with an electrical detonator and a time-release attachment. Of course, you don't know if dynamite even comes in various "grades" or what the hell an electrical detonator is, but that doesn't matter because nobody else does, either. All they know is you sound like somebody who knows what the hell he's talking about and they'll react favorably.

You can also have fun by tying a road flare to an old alarm clock mechanism and secreting the thing in an abandoned locker. Arrange to "discover" it and report it to the authorities. They'll evacuate the building and summon the bomb squad and waste half the afternoon before finding out it's all a hoax and you'll have a laugh at their expense.

A word of caution, though: If they catch your ass planting phony bombs and scaring the shit out of everybody, some pissed-off judge will send you away at state expense for a long rest. People don't like bombs, real or imagined, and you'll need a reincarnated Clarence Darrow to keep your ass out of the hoosegow.

In reality, though, bomb threats don't work that well. Nobody takes them seriously since damn few people are actually crazy enough to plant real bombs around the neighborhood. At Cody, we had a code word that was used to alert the staff that there was a bomb threat but nobody left the building.

They'd announce over the PA that a mythical Mr. Peabody was wanted in the office and everybody (including the kids) knew that meant we'd had a bomb threat. Teachers would saunter out into the halls and rummage through the empty lockers and generally dilly-dally around for a few minutes and everybody would forget all about it and go back to work.

Just another word on the subject and we'll move on to other things. Bomb threats are not only ineffective but they're also a bit dumb. A timely false fire alarm at least has the advantage of providing the school with a useful evacuation drill and may even help saves lives when the place really does catch on fire, but a bomb threat just irritates people and will only be ignored in the end.

Besides, people who make bomb threats are usually regarded as half-wits and ignorant assholes by one and all, and rightly so. You don't need those labels since your personal standing in the community is already lower than sea level and being known as a mad bomber will do nothing to enhance it.

## Chapter Twenty-Six

### Lying

Everyone is familiar with the George Washington and the cherry tree fairy tale because teachers and parents have been using it for years to instill the dubious virtue of honesty in young people, but I'm here to tell you it's a lot of crap. People everywhere decry lying and assert that one should always be honest and tell the truth but they don't believe it themselves for a minute and, what's more, they never practice such madness in their own lives.

Actually, lying is a very useful skill, one that will stand you in good stead everywhere and at all times. Suppose your teacher shows up wearing a new cheap hairpiece that makes him look like a complete dope and he asks you how you like it. If you tell him the truth you'll hurt the poor sap's feelings and he'll repay you by failing your ass and making you take English over again and all because you bought that cherry tree crap.

Or suppose you spend an evening scoring with little Amy from your math class and when you get home your mother asks what you've been doing. Only a total moron would say, "I cannot tell a lie, Mother, I've been laying little Amy."

I mean, Jesus Christ, be reasonable here. The situation calls for a first-class lie told with skill and verve both to protect little Amy's honor and to save your ass from being grounded until you're out of college.

What about the moral question of lying? Forget it, everybody else does. It's a non-issue. Everybody lies and they do it all the time. It boils down to a case of situational ethics, i.e., when you're in a situation where lying will save you from some gross inconvenience or benefit you in some direct way, lie.

That's how the rest of the world deals with it. Lying is so ingrained most people would lie when the truth would better serve them. Who are you to go against such a well-established custom?

However, there's an art to lying, one I didn't really learn until I started teaching in Detroit. The secret is to make up a story and stick to it no matter what. Never waver. If overwhelming evidence indicates you're lying, insist there's a conspiracy against you. Hint that there are aspects of the story that will be revealed at the "right time" that will vindicate you. This gambit worked for that asshole Sen. McCarthy, remember?

Assume an injured air. Offer to take an oath on a Bible—don't worry, nobody will ever actually go get a Bible; besides, most people wouldn't know where to find one on short notice, anyway. If somebody does whip out a Bible, go ahead and swear on it, as it will only make your lie look more credible.

Demand a lie detector test and insist that the other guy take one, too. This is an especially good ploy since they're not about to bring in an expensive piece of machinery just to find out whether you really did your homework or are lying about it. What's more, even if they did everybody knows the things are unreliable and don't mean anything.

In other words, never admit you're not telling the truth. If you're caught red-handed, swear you didn't do it. If you stick to your story long enough people begin to entertain doubts and they eventually get tired of the whole thing and give up. Consider the following scenario at Cody.

I walk into a classroom and see a kid writing on the teacher's bulletin board with a magic marker.

"Hey!" I shout. "What the hell are you doing?"

The kid whirls around. "I ain't doin' nothin'!" he lies.

"What?! Why, you little creep, I just saw you writing on the wall with that magic marker!"

"It ain't me!" he says. "I jus' found this here marker an' I seen the board was marked up an' I was seein' do it match the writin'." He turns to his accomplices—the other kids in the class. "Ain't that right, Jose?"

"Yeah," Jose lies.

"Billy's tellin' the truth," another swears.

The others nod and look solemn.

"Oh, yeah?" I say. "Then how do you explain your signature being on the wall?"

"What?!" Billy says. "How'd my name get up there, man? Somebody mus' of forged it. Ain't this some shit?" Etc.

And there you have it. Billy had magic marker ink all over his fingers, his handwritten signature was scrawled across the wall, and I had seen him actually engaged in the crime, but he swore he was innocent and never changed his story. What the hell could I do short of grabbing the little fraud by the throat and shaking the shit out of him?

That's dedicated lying, professional lying, inspired lying. I learned a lesson myself and it's come in handy on various occasions since then.

So don't listen to the moralizers out there, as they're hypocrites and mental bankrupts. Lying to save one's ass is a time-honored practice, one that's diligently followed all over the world, and you should have no compunction about telling lies big and small every chance you get.

Remember the liars' code: Make up a story and stick to it no matter what!

## Chapter Twenty-Seven

### Parking

If you have a car and go to a school where parking is limited, the best place to park is in the teachers' lot. Of course, the teachers don't want you in their parking lot because you take up spaces they need themselves and, besides, they don't want you stealing their hubcaps and multi-band radios. In order to keep your unwelcome ass the hell out of their lot, the school issues parking decals that are affixed to the windshield and only cars so adorned can park in the restricted lot.

One way for you to beat this dodge is to steal a parking decal and put it on your own windshield, and you can do this by stealing one from a teacher's car. Since these decals are usually hard to get off the glass intact, it may be easier to just steal the teacher's windshield and replace yours with the new one.

You can also find a kid who works around the office and has access to the decals and have him swipe one for you. Better yet, you can infiltrate the office yourself and set up a nice little business selling decals, doctored transcripts, phony diplomas, pre-stamped hall passes, and so on.

Another ruse that works is to put a piece of paper on your windshield with the words SUBSTITUTE TEACHER written on it. Since subs don't usually have parking decals, the authorities will usually take your phony claim at face value and hassle some other poor slob who didn't have the foresight to read this book.

But the best ploy of all is the easiest to work and it produces first-rate results. Suppose your school uses green decals with black numerals on them. Okay. All you have to do is get a piece of green paper or cardboard the same size and shade of green and draw some numbers on it with a black magic marker and put it on your windshield. From a distance an observer will only see the green color and assume it's a regular decal.

Sure, if they get right up on it and peer at it from a distance of a four or five feet they'll spot the counterfeit, but not one teacher in a thousand will ever think to scrutinize the thing that closely. This ruse works on the same principle as the hall pass scam mentioned earlier where you merely carry a piece of paper in your hand and boldly wave it at any challengers. People will accept it for what it's supposed to be.

Don't forget the major premise for surviving in this world: it runs on bullshit.

## Chapter Twenty-Eight

### Extortionists/Bullies

This section will be of special interest to you if you go to school in Detroit or one of the other big cities in the country. In fact, you can encounter extortionists in schools large and small everywhere. Surely, everyone runs into one or more of these assholes in school and has to surrender his lunch money or brand-new baseball glove to avoid elaborate dental work or worse.

It's especially bad in big city schools, though, because a lot of the kids who go to these schools would be serving time somewhere if there were any justice at all in our society. Instead, they're hanging around the halls and johns waiting for you to show up with that lunch money or new glove.

These guys are always ignorant assholes. They have an IQ about on a par with the average goldfish and probably resort to extortion because they're not smart enough to learn how to wrap hamburgers at McDonald's. They fail at everything they take in school, hardly ever go to class, get suspended four or five times a semester, can't read or spell or write or count all the way to a hundred, and they're generally ugly, as well.

Most of them aren't even very big or tough. They compensate for these deficiencies by traveling in gangs and arming themselves with wicked looking knives and/or revolvers. Their modus operandi is simplicity itself; they approach the unwary and order him to "check it in, motherfucker," a phrase that replaces the outdated "stick 'em up, motherfucker."

Such a scene might go something like this. A simple-minded dude shows up on campus wearing a brand-new pair of hundred-dollar Nikes and is instantly spotted by the local extortionist and his associates.

"Hey, man, them's nice shoes you got there," one says.

"Yeah," his accomplice says, "you better check 'em in, man."

"What?" says the simple-minded dude. (I told you he was slow; only the slowest of the slow would wear such shoes to school in the first place.)

"Gimme them shoes, motherfucker!" the extortionist explains. He pulls a switchblade machete from his pocket to encourage cooperation and the dude has no option but to hand over the shoes before the asshole gets any more confused than he already is and severs an artery for him.

Or what about the bullies? Every school has them and they're easy to spot. Always big and thick skulled with beady eyes and limited vocabularies, they have a penchant for violence—if the victim is small and weak enough so he won't pose any threat to the bully. Bullies never fight guys their own size because they're essentially cowards at heart.

Anyway, what can you do about such violence done to you and your possessions? Obviously, you can't resist. You also can't report the crazy bastards to the authorities because they'll only be released on their own recognizance within fifteen minutes and guess whom they'll come looking for? Is there, in fact, anything you can do?

Of course there is. For one thing you've read this book and know that brains triumph over brawn every time, and, besides, Grandpa Ganja is going to offer several practical suggestions that will help you deal with them.

For openers, you can always join up with them. Befriend some of the smarter ones, tell them you've always admired extortionists and have long wanted to be one yourself. Gain their confidence. Once they accept you as a bona-fide convert to ignorance and depravity, you can find out where they store their booty and you'll be able to pick out a new pair of Nikes even better than the ones you lost.

I know, this plan not only requires that you hang around with these assholes, but you also have to pretend you actually enjoy their company and that's hard to do. All conversations will be monosyllabic, you'll never hear an idea that couldn't be fully understood by any mature cat, and you'll have to gaze on their ugly mugs for hours at a time without throwing up.

Come to think of it, you might be better off if you just forgot about those sneakers and got on with your life.

But don't despair, as there are other courses of action open to the enterprising guy with revenge on his mind. Suppose there's a particular crook or bully in your school and you want to get his ass. Find out where the asshole has his locker, fill a squirt gun with red ink, and shoot it into the locker through the air vents. When he finds all his worldly goods covered with red ink he'll fume and curse and flail the air and threaten to get the dude who did it while you lurk nearby and enjoy the spectacle.

Make up a note using letters cut from newspapers the way kidnappers do and tell the asshole one of his victims was responsible. Let him know why he's under attack but leave no clues leading to you for obvious reasons. Sign it with a skull and crossbones in red ink and pin it to the locker for all to see. Warn him there's more to come.

If the thug has a car slash all his tires and leave another note signed in red ink. He'll have to go out and steal four more tires and he'll be pissed in the extreme.

Still another idea is to slip a joint into his coat pocket and then anonymously tip the principal that the guy's carrying dope. They'll kick his ass out of school for as long as a whole week and add another page to his already voluminous file at headquarters. Be sure to provide the usual note signed in red ink.

Spread rumors around school that he and his entire gang have clap and herpes. Urge all girls who've been within ten feet of them to get a series of shots and never give the losers any more no matter what. Get a job helping in the lunchroom and piss on his hamburger and fries. Be sure to send along the note later so he'll know he's been had. Put a wad of well-chewed bubble gum on his seat and ruin the new pants he just stole yesterday. Carve his name in the new desktop and see that the teacher finds it.

In short, use your imagination. Enlist the aid of your friends. A concerted effort could easily drive the stupid bastard and his equally stupid pals out of school and into the lawless streets where they belong. It's true that none of this will actually help you get your sneakers back, but you'll get a tremendous amount of satisfaction in knowing that you've struck a blow for justice and fair play and helped rid your school of a bunch of ignorant assholes.

## Chapter Twenty-Nine

### Class Schedules

This chapter is one of the most crucial ones in the book. Every high school student in America knows the importance of getting a decent schedule of classes, one that lets him start at a reasonable hour—say about noon—and finish up no later than two-thirty. What you usually get, of course, is a schedule that starts shortly after dawn and doesn't end until dusk has covered the landscape all the way up to the Arctic Circle.

And the length of the schedule is only one source of concern; it also makes a difference what courses you end up with. Suppose you sign up for French and all the French classes are full. Fine. The computer substitutes Mandarin Chinese and you're stuck with a class you don't want and can't possibly pass. Or you ask for the journalism elective and get wood shop instead. Or an elementary arithmetic class is inexplicably changed to something called Calculus 8. Or...but you get the picture.

Still another consideration is the teacher you get. Everybody knows some teachers are harder than others—or crazier or homelier or all three—and such teachers are to be avoided at all costs. The teacher who has a reputation for failing 80% of her senior class is not somebody you want to get involved with. And the teacher who's already had your brother(s) and/or sister(s) and knows your family to be made up entirely of half-wits and dunderheads is likely to hold you in low esteem right from the start and is definitely one to be avoided.

On the other hand Old Man Fogarty, who gives everybody an A and doesn't believe in homework, is the man you want for your math teacher. And Senile Smithers, who loses all her records every semester and has to let the kids mark themselves, is your obvious choice for senior English. It's clearly imperative that you have some say in the matter of whom your teachers will be if you expect to survive the coming semester.

Okay, how do you go about getting a good schedule? Well, there are a number of dodges tried and true that will practically let you dictate your own schedule—or at least get you one you can live with. For starters, there's the throw-away-your-schedule-and-start-over ploy.

It works like this. Suppose you go through the whole registration process and end up with a dreadful schedule. You get all the wrong classes and all the wrong teachers and it runs from dawn to dusk. Just throw the thing away and go through the whole process again. Of course, you'll end up registered in two completely different programs, but by the time this gets out they'll let you stay in the program you've been attending and they'll drop you from the other one.

Will they be pissed? Sure, but so what?

You can always get an early schedule and get

out of school somewhere around noon by lying and claiming you have a job. Insist that you are the sole support for your widowed mother and numerous siblings and must be out early for your job at the pizzeria. Sprinkle some flour in your hair and have an anchovy stuck to your textbook. This one never fails.

Another successful strategy is to start going to the class you want and skip the one assigned to you. Tell the teacher there must be some mistake and you'll see your counselor right away and straighten it all out. Keep going to that class and stall her as long as possible. Once they sort it out you'll keep the class you're attending because it's easier that way.

Then there's the Divide and Conquer Gambit. This successful plan involves going to the teacher whose class you want and asking if there's room in it for another student. Tell her your counselor asked you to find out. No, she won't check with the counselor. Have her jot down a note saying she does have space left. Take the note back to the registration area and use it as proof that Senile Smithers wants you to have her class and they'll make the change.

Well, these ploys will help you get a good schedule, but the best scheme of all involves your parents. Go home and bitch to your folks about the lousy schedule you got and tell them to raise Cain with the school. If they'll write a note demanding the desired changes, eight out of ten school officials will immediately give in and change the thing for you. And if your parents will go to the school and demand consideration, the remaining 20% of them will back down, as well.

This plan rests on the well-known fact that school administrators are essentially spineless individuals without the moral courage to stand up to an indignant field mouse. The average administrator is intimidated by any taxpayer with enough balls to tell him where to head in, and especially if said taxpayer threatens to go to the school board and report his ass for assorted crimes and misdemeanors. The point is you don't have to accept a schedule just because they say you must.

Think creatively. Work the angles. You have absolutely nothing to lose since the penalty for being caught in any of these schemes is no more than some sort of vague warning about following rules, etc.

In other words, if you end with a screwed-up schedule, you have only yourself to blame.

## Chapter Thirty

### In-School Sales — Be An Entrepreneur

I don't know about your school, but Cody High is a veritable sales mecca for assorted commercial interests. They sell all sorts of stuff in the halls and classrooms and around the campus. Every teacher, club, or department that decides it needs revenue to finance its latest boondoggle sponsors these sales.

The home ec department might want a new microwave oven, say, and they sponsor a sale of cupcakes which they peddle all over the place and interfere as much as possible with what little education is going on in the joint. Or the wood shop might need some lumber and they take to the halls with raffle tickets or some such thing and disrupt any order the home ec people missed.

When the foreign language department needs money for more cassette tapes they sell boxes of chocolate candy and the PTA is forever holding bake sales in front of the school office with the result that half the student body is late for class because they stop to buy some jelly donuts. What's more, they eat the damn things in the halls and classrooms and johns and leave crumbs everywhere and the mice and roaches proliferate as a result.

But the chief offender and leading disrupter of

the general order is the phys ed department. It seems these guys are forever running out of basketballs or in dire need of new football uniforms and they'll launch a new potato chip campaign. Actually, they launched a potato chip campaign in the fall of 1942 or so and the damn thing has gone on uninterrupted ever since.

Hordes of kids are sent out into the halls with huge clear plastic sacks chock full of potato chips in little bags. They hawk the things up and down the halls and draw large crowds of kids at every corner who clog up the halls and create a jam that keeps others from getting through so they can go to class. They even sell the damn things in class, often when the teacher is busily trying to drum some sense into their vacant heads.

Naturally, the teachers complain mightily because all this crap keeps the place in turmoil and wreaks havoc with their attempts to get some teaching done, but nobody is willing to put a stop to such lucrative enterprises. To this very day a visitor to Cody will be offered a twenty-cent jelly donut for a buck or a bag of ten-cent potato chips for fifty cents within minutes of entering the building.

I guess education is all right in its place, but Mammon comes first in our schools just as it does everywhere else.

This situation could be turned into a profitable one for a bright and quick-thinking lad with dreams of entrepreneurship dancing in his greedy little head. All he has to do is get his own large plastic sack and fill it up with potato chips and sell them at triple their cost to his classmates. Everybody will assume he's selling them for the phys ed department and he'll make a fortune.

A really enterprising lad could branch out into Indian jewelry and candy and T-shirts and a host of other products. A freshman could end up with a mini-empire by the time he became a senior and even stay on after graduation and make a career out of in-school sales. Such an entrepreneur might even set franchises up in other schools and go public and get written up in Forbes.

Anyway, even without the empire it's a good way to make some ready cash with very little effort. Of course, I'll expect a generous commission for coming up with the idea.

After all, isn't that the American way?

## Chapter Thirty-One

### The Cafeteria

Why can't they run a successful school lunch program with decent food and an atmosphere conducive to enjoying what one eats? It happens that almost all school cafeterias are unpopular with the kids who have to eat there—and with good reason. For one, consider the matter of ambience.

How the hell can anyone enjoy a meal in a cavernous room with tiled walls and floors which allow sound waves to ricochet all over the place like a lot of marbles in a spinning steel drum? The noise level in the average school cafeteria is hardly distinguishable from a busy foundry. Everyone screams since normal speaking tones are out of the question because nobody would hear them.

After three-quarters of an hour in such a place most kids go back to class with nervous tics and may have to stop off in the john and smoke something to settle down.

Then there's the matter of the food. One sees menus listing marble-hard whole kernel corn, flat-tasting green beans, gooey mashed potatoes, rubber hot dogs in crumbly buns that have been carefully sliced on impossible angles, and other mysterious dishes whose identity is known to no one. The adjectives above don't appear on the menu, of course, but they should.

The one thing these so-called foods have going for them is that they're nutritious and constitute a balanced diet, but what good is that if nobody eats the stuff? Have you ever watched as the kids leave your cafeteria and dump uneaten food into the garbage? I'm not sure how such a thing could happen, but I've heard there's sometimes more food thrown into the garbage than was served during a given lunch.

Naturally, everybody is concerned about this situation but nobody seems to know exactly what to do about it. Some schools have even started serving fast food stuff like hamburgers and fries and fish sandwiches but with only limited success. Let's face it, the average school hamburger isn't going to be mistaken for a Big Mac and the Colonel refuses to give them his secret recipe.

There are some things you can do to protect yourself from ptomaine poisoning but the choices aren't many. The obvious one is don't eat cafeteria food. Bring your lunch. Throw a peanut butter and jelly sandwich and an apple into a brown paper sack and you'll have a quality lunch no school lunchroom in the country can match. Naturally, the wiser ones among you will find a way to trick their mothers into making their sandwiches.

Another option is to get a job working in the kitchen. This will give you access to the food before the cooks get their hands on it and you'll be able to eat it before it's defiled. Still, the hot dogs will be rubber and the mashed potatoes gooey—unless you eat them raw. You can make cheese sandwiches, though, before the cooks concoct their notorious macaroni and cheese that's completely inedible, and there's bound to be a jar of peanut butter around somewhere.

In fact, you might even be able to eat what the cooks eat (surely they don't eat the same stuff they serve you!) but it's not likely since they eat later in the backroom where no one can see them grilling inch-thick steaks and passing the beluga caviar around.

But the easiest plan of all is to go out for lunch. Sneak off to the nearest pizza parlor or hamburger joint and have a burger and some edible fries washed down with a liter or two of Pepsi. You could be eating a more wholesome diet, it's true, but at least you'll be able to hear yourself think there and you won't have to put up with the tension and anxiety of the school cafeteria. You might even win a free car or something in one of the contests these places are always running, and you sure as hell won't be winning any cars at school.

One caveat here, though. If you skip out for an illicit lunch of Big Macs and fries there's a damn good chance you'll be seen by half-a-dozen of your teachers because that's where they go to eat. And they won't even have to turn you in because the principal will probably be sitting at the next table.

## Chapter Thirty-Two

### APPLE POLISHERS

Call them whatever you like, we all know what they are. Ear bangers, ass kissers, teacher's pet, sycophants, and assholes generally who spend all their time currying favor from people who aren't worthy of the attention. They're everywhere, bowing and scraping and living life on their knees in hopes of getting better grades or a pay raise or recognition or some other transient reward when they should be standing tall and laughing at life for the ephemeral and transitory thing it is.

Everybody dislikes these types. It makes real people uneasy to see somebody blatantly kissing ass, especially since they're always looking for some advantage over others (you) in the process. They're afraid to meet you man-to-man in a fair fight; they'd rather suck up to the teacher for an A than pitch in and earn the thing honorably.

(On the other hand, remember our goal here. If you're without options and your life depends on that A, why, the end justifies the means, as Machiavelli would have it. So flatter away.)

Still, I have disheartening news for you: it's the ass kissers who run things out there and one of these days you'll be working for them. I know it's a dreadful thought but it's also true. The creeps you see around school with the brown rings on their noses will be your bosses because society holds a special place for those who are willing to sell out and go through life without a shred of dignity or pride.

If you are determined to succeed in life and don't care what you think of yourself, learn to kneel. Laugh at your teacher's dumb jokes, sit up front and smile and nod, be a row monitor, wash her blackboard and dust her erasers, frown when she frowns and learn to cluck your tongue disapprovingly as she does. In short, flatter her ass.

If you learn these traits well enough in high school, you'll practically be assured unlimited success in the real world later on. Every boss loves a properly trained yes man who knows how and when to grovel. They're susceptible to flattery of the most egregious kind and never tire of hearing themselves praised. The quality of your work is never as important to these arrant fools as whether or not they find you sufficiently cowed and humble.

Ask anyone with experience in the real world if this isn't the case. We all know countless people who were among the least able employees and yet rose to positions of grandeur based solely on their ability to suck up to their betters.

You can see examples of this in your own school. As we've seen, the principal didn't get his job because he was smarter than the rest of the teachers or a better worker or better qualified; he got the job because he insinuated himself into the superintendent's good graces. It's a truism everywhere, and the sooner you find it out the sooner you'll be able to deal with the bastards on an even basis.

It's a common mistake for young people without experience in the real world to think they can succeed by merit alone. They earn two or three degrees in esoteric fields and willingly put in twelve-hour days and lug work home on weekends and are shocked when the promotions go to the boss's relatives or somebody's friend or some asshole hollering about how he was robbed of his civil rights or some such crap.

Well, in the best of all possible worlds merit will be rewarded, but I'm afraid we're not living in such a place now. Keep an eye on the apple polishers and you'll see what I mean.

## Chapter Thirty-Three

### DRUGS

Every teenager is faced with some heavy decisions to make about the various substances out there that will seriously alter his view of reality and even undermine life itself—and make it impossible to survive high school. Nancy Reagan offered a panacea, of course: just say no.

But that's easier to do when you're an old lady in the White House without the normal drives and uncontrollable juices of a swiftly moving modern American teenager living in a brand-new world wide open to those with the balls to partake of its wonders. In other words, you.

Fortunately, you have the advantage of Grandpa Ganja's keen insight into the subject, insight acquired by decades of careful study and time spent on Mt. Fuji with Zen monks who know everything and taught me how to roll a proper Zen joint.

First, let's start with one of the worst drugs out there, the one that does the most damage. That's right, tobacco. The stuff kills 400,000 Americans every year and puts a lot more on waiting lists for new lungs. It even says so on the pack, for God's sake. Are all smokers illiterate? Or idiots? Somebody should make a study of smokers and see how many points below normal their IQs are.

So, how dumb are you? Can't you read the pack? Somebody offers you a cigarette and you take it? You think it's chic or sophisticated? Or cool? Grandpa Ganja did, once. I smoked cigarettes and switched to cigars and finally got wise twenty-five years ago and quit smoking altogether.

Well, not altogether, but mostly.

I shouldn't have to tell you this but I will. Don't use tobacco in any form. It really can kill you.

What about alcohol, or, more specifically, beer? Everybody knows there's no point in lecturing teenagers on beer drinking. Most teenagers know all about beer drinking and a hell of a lot of them are already experts in the field.

What teenager hasn't gone to a party where everybody drank beer and got sick and regurgitated all over the place? Or gone on a picnic and bobbed for mysterious objects in vats of foaming beer? Or sneaked into a bar with phony ID and downed a few schooners of the stuff?

Drinking beer in America is one of the chief rites of passage for adolescents, a custom long since established as immutable and one that's violated only by the nerdiest of nerds. I think it's harmless in itself if done in moderation, but that's a big "if." What one wants to remember is that beer is an alcoholic beverage and alcohol is real tricky stuff. In fact, alcohol will cause your ass more trouble than all the drugs in the world if you aren't careful.

Nancy Reagan deplored drugs but she still

served alcohol in the White House. Maybe nobody told her about the ten million alcoholics out there whose lives have been all but obliterated by booze.

It's even more of a threat to you because it's legal, you can get it anywhere for a modest cost, and there's no social stigma attached to drinking it. It's even considered chic, especially among kids who haven't the sense to know better.

Alcohol, then, is dangerous stuff. It sneaks up on you and gets a lock on your liver and before you know it you're a derelict on skid row or worse. I say have the first beer for thirst and the second one for taste. Don't have any more.

The same goes for alcohol in booze and wine. The stuff will kill you—or make you wish you were dead. Try to avoid it. Drinking isn't clever or cute of macho or anything else, but it can be dumb.

Develop a taste for all these sugar-free drinks they have nowadays and pour Nutra-Sweet into your body by the gallon. While you may very well get three or four different kinds of cancers from all that chemical crap, at least you won't be a candidate for AA membership.

One more point to consider. Not only shouldn't you drink and drive, you shouldn't let any other asshole drive drunk with you in the car. If the driver is sloshed, get out and walk. Don't worry about looking like a dork to your friends or not being "cool."

The dorks are the ones who stay in the car with some half-wit behind the wheel who's plastered.

You can often see these guys in the county morgue, a place where it's pretty hard to look cool even with the lowered temperatures one finds there.

So, easy on the alcohol.

Now on to the illegal drugs. A simple rule: avoid the ones that are addictive. Which ones are addictive? All of them are with one exception. Everyone knows heroin is treacherous and evil and only unstable types will muck about with it. Fortunately, you won't see much heroin around the average high school since it's a drug for the really desperate and most teenagers aren't in that league.

The rule here is simple: Don't sniff heroin, drink it, inject it, smoke it, inhale it, or remain in a room where it's present. The people who use it are the very last people on Earth you want to number among your acquaintances, as hanging out with heroin addicts might easily turn you into one.

Besides, heroin can kill you the very first time you use it. That's reason enough.

Cocaine is also addictive. They say it's not quite as bad as heroin but it's bad enough that you don't need it. Coke can melt your nose, cause the heebie-jeebies, and lower IQs. It's also expensive as you build a tolerance to it and require ever more to satisfy your addiction. Give cocaine a pass and you'll be glad you did.

Of course, if you grow up to become a stockbroker on Wall Street you may have to use cocaine just to prove you belong, but nobody else should use it.

And whatever you do, avoid crack. Why? Because the government uses the legal system to help warehouse undesirables (people of color) by sentencing crack users for terms five times as long as coke users. You will get five years for possession of five grams of crack and one year for five hundred grams of coke!

Since almost all cocaine users are white and almost all crack users are people of color, such wildly disparate sentences can only be seen as a means of controlling potential troublemakers by getting them off the streets for a few years.

How can such a thing happen in the land of the free?

How about prescription drugs? They're fine as long as a doctor prescribes them—and I mean your doctor, not your uncle's. But remember, all pain pills are addictive. They'll do your ass in if you abuse them so don't. Avoid people who do.

And now for marijuana. As you might expect, anybody called Grandpa Ganja might have some vague connection to weed and you'd be right. I am one of the most qualified experts on the planet when pot is the subject, and not because I studied it in school.

In fact, I have smoked pot every day for over thirty-six years to treat my glaucoma and I know what it looks, smells, and tastes like and how the stuff works, as well as any man.

In keeping with my avowed plan to stick to the truth insofar as such a thing is possible, I must say that marijuana is utterly harmless. Pot cannot hurt you. The only way pot could hurt you would be if a bale of it fell off a high shelf and broke your neck. It won't fry your brain or turn you into a lazy bum or addict you or ruin your relationships or lead to harder drugs.

Think about it. If pot fries one's brain, how could I have written this brilliant book?

Pot doesn't incapacitate you to the point where you'll drive your car into a wall the way a fifth of Johnny Walker will, and it won't make you sick and cause you to regurgitate on your girlfriend's best dress. The stuff is fairly cheap, at least when compared to the outrageous cost of other drugs, and it's less illegal than the others.

What does "less illegal" mean? It means they won't throw your ass in the hoosegow for consecutive life sentences for using it. The crime of dope smoking is a misdemeanor in most states—and it's even legal in some places like California and Arizona where you can legally grow it for your own use as medicine. Even more, some places like Denver and the state of Alaska have legalized marijuana for personal use by anyone of legal age.

On the other hand, read the papers. People are being sent to the big house for unbelievable stretches when harder drugs are involved. Some poor sap sells a tenth-of-an-ounce of crack and he gets 15 to 50 years for it. Contrarily, you can have a bucketful of grass and get on-the-spot probation and maybe a small fine.

Does that mean you should hurry out and buy

a bag of dope and rent space in the school john? Of course not. If marijuana isn't a harmful substance, it also isn't likely to do you a whole lot of good, either—unless you're sick. In that case, pot might easily help in restoring your health, as its medicinal benefits are well known. It follows obviously that you are the only one who knows whether or not you're sick.

For the record, Grandpa Ganja does not recommend young people smoking pot. I'm so against it, in fact, that I'm willing to go a step further and help you get off the stuff at great personal sacrifice.

I figure you won't smoke if you don't have any stash, so I want all teenage tokers out there to send their pot to me and I'll personally burn the stuff up for you. Just put it in a plain envelope and send it to me via UPS. I'm in the book.

Oh, if you have any clips or papers or the odd Tommy Chong collectible pipe, why, send them along too as you won't need them anymore

In any case, I thought you should know the truth for once instead of being lied to by so-called experts who lump all drugs together and issue dire warnings about all of them without real accuracy, but that doesn't mean you should start your own marijuana farm.

The fact is that marijuana will get your ass fired from just about any job in the country if the boss finds the stuff in your urine. It's common practice for security guys to sneak up on people in the john with bottle in hand to catch them in mid-stream, as it were. It won't be long before one hit on a joint will start bells ringing all over the place and the hittee will be surrounded by cops and frowning bosses before he knows what hit him.

One more. A pot conviction on your record could make you ineligible for government loans for education and you'll have to go to a community college instead of Stanford. Caveat emptor.

So it looks like you'll be a lot better off in the long run if you go easy on all this stuff. Life's hard enough as it is without hanging a drug problem on your ass. Whatever you do, though, try to act responsibly and intelligently and know exactly what you're doing.

Let me sum up, then, the rules for surviving the hazards of using mind-altering substances during your high school career—or ever. Drink beer moderately, wine only with meals in better restaurants, and hard booze not at all. Avoid all hard drugs. Take no prescription drugs unless the prescription comes from your own doctor.

Do not smoke cigarettes or use tobacco in any form. While marijuana in moderation won't kill you, it's a good idea to leave it alone at least until you finish high school and/or college and have moved to Denver.

And there you have it, sound advice, honest advice, advice with some practical value attached to it that will work in the real world where you happen to live.

## Chapter Thirty-Four

### Hall Lockers

Getting a good locker is important for the sake of convenience if nothing else. If all your classes are on the third-floor up front, you don't want a locker on the first-floor in the rear. Ideally, you want a locker that's centrally located so you won't have to run like hell all the time to avoid being late to class. Besides, with a good locker location you'll have all that much more time to lounge around in the halls between classes or duck into the john for a quick smoke or whatever.

Some lockers carry more prestige than others. A locker down near the gym is to be avoided because you'll have a bunch of ignorant jocks hanging around all the time. And one near the wood shop is as bad since that's where all the black leather jacket dudes hang out and all that sawdust and crap will leak into your locker and get on your stuff and people will think you're a shop major.

What to do? Easy. Offer to help the teacher in charge of locker distribution. Once you get your hands on the forms you can assign yourself any locker you like. In fact, the secret then is to assign yourself several lockers in various parts of the building so no matter where you are in the school you won't be more than fifteen steps from one of your lockers.

You can even rent out locker space. Sign up for

lockers by the dozen in choice locations and lease them to your classmates. Or charge them a fee to give them a locker where they want one. You can even assign enemies to the most undesirable lockers in the school, the ones with busted doors and missing shelves.

Word will quickly spread that you're the one to see about locker accommodations and you'll soon realize the advantages of power in this world. You'll be invited to all the big parties and cheerleaders will vie with each other to go out with you and you'll be encouraged to run for class president. After that it's just a step to Congress and a prosperous life of rapine and graft and insider stock trading.

And all this because you had the presence of mind to insinuate yourself into a position of power. Aren't you glad you read this book now?

## Chapter Thirty-Five

### Senior Trips

It's never too early to start thinking about your senior trip. Even if you're a freshman and you can't conceive of four whole years ever passing in your lifetime, pass they will and you'll find your senior trip is a guided tour of some local theme park unless you plan ahead to avoid such a catastrophe.

You see, school authorities like to plan "safe" senior trips, trips that won't result in lawsuits and unwanted pregnancies and scandals harmful to their own well-being. Accordingly, they want you to take a Greyhound bus trip to Mammoth Cave, or do Disneyland, or motor out to the Grand Canyon, or go to D.C. and have your picture taken at the Lincoln Memorial. In other words, they want you in a controlled setting where they're the ones with control.

They also try to load you up with chaperones, usually at a ratio of one for every two kids. They know instinctively there's no way in hell you can get in any trouble, i.e., have any fun, if there are enough people around to watch your ass.

And, what's more, they always pick real winners like the local clergyman who frowns on dancing and equates copping a feel with mass murder or some broken-down assistant principal who wears bloomers and blushes at bra ads on TV. The only worse choice would be your own parents.

The truth is you want a senior trip to a place where you'll be exposed to sin and evil, a place where you can see naked women and drink that third beer and experience some of the seamier side of life. It's too bad they closed down Sodom and Gomorrah since these would have been ideal sites, but you still have Las Vegas and Atlantic City and Club Med (the one where they don't wear clothes).

After all, aren't you young adults now? Isn't that what graduating from high school is all about, the changing of adolescents into grown-ups who are ready to take their rightful places in the larger world?

Of course it is, and that's what you tell them. You want to go to the same places where your parents and teachers go for vacations. If naked women and gambling and drinking champagne from ladies' slippers are good enough for them they're good enough for you, too.

Form up committees, stage rallies, send for brochures, volunteer to head a research team to check out hotel accommodations in Vegas, start an overall tan so you won't look funny when you hit the Club Med beaches in your birthday suit.

The point is you must make your plans early. Even now a lot of old bats and Sunday school superintendents and assistant principals are planning to send you on that Mammoth Cave trip and you have to head them off at the pass, so to speak. Let them know you've got your heart set on Vegas and that you won't settle for anything less than a full ration of depravity and riotous living.

In other words, demand that they treat you as the young adults you really are and give you some say in where you take that well-earned senior trip. After all, whose senior trip is it, anyway?

## Chapter Thirty-Six

### THE PROM

Hey, you only get one prom, right? Most colleges don't have them, except for a few aberrations like West Point, and who the hell wants to go through four years of that crap just to go to a dance?

Proms are important, prom night is a class event, and you'll want to plan well ahead for yours. Start saving in your freshman year. Try to get better looking by your senior year so you can get a date. Work the angles. Remember, the race belongs to the swift—unless you allow for affirmative action.

The thing is to get an early start. It's crucial that you get an acceptable date for the prom, one that will complement you and add to your social standing among your peers. Of course, the girls aren't stupid, they're also looking for dates that will add to their social standing and the chances are pretty good that will mean trouble for the likes of you.

There are ways around that for the more alert ones out there. One sure-fire scheme is to prey on the known weaknesses of the so-called fair sex. We all know that girls are motivated by such things as a guy's financial standing, that they're attracted to the guy with the great car and designer clothes and a general aura of success. Okay, you capitalize on that by circulating rumors at the start of your senior year that you're in line to inherit a massive fortune from a rich relative who lives on another continent.

Be seen leafing through travel brochures and pamphlets listing villas for sale on assorted romantic seacoasts. Lug around copies of Forbes Magazine and the Wall Street Journal. When questioned about your impending good fortune, smile cryptically and be subtly evasive.

In no time at all every nymphet on the cheerleading squad will be fawning over you like a servile would-be heir lusting after a rich relative's favor. You'll assume an indifferent air, of course, and thereby make yourself even more desirable. If you play your cards right you should be able to run amuck among the prettiest girls on campus in your senior year before finally settling on the lucky girl you'll take to the prom.

You girls can play the same game, of course, since guys are just as avaricious as you are. The star quarterback will certainly look on you in a more favorable light if he thinks you'll be worth millions some day or have an uncle who scouts for the Big Ten. You make up both the millions and the uncle, of course, and hoist the sap with his own petard.

Another dodge that works also deals with the known fact that girls are practical creatures when it comes to dispensing their favors. As we all know, the average guy will accommodate just about any girl who makes herself available and will invariably end up marrying some sloe-eyed creature solely because she has great boobs, but girls are a lot cagier than that. If they're going to dispense any favors, they want at least reasonable prospects of getting something tangible in return.

Accordingly, in your senior year tell everybody you've been accepted at Harvard Law School and anticipate a brilliant legal career with a prestigious New York law firm that your uncle heads up. You will instantly be regarded as a "good catch" (yes, girls actually use such phrases!) and even the more comely girls will respond favorably to your overtures.

Incidentally, their mothers are also girls and think like them and will be delighted that their daughters are going out with a future New York lawyer. You may have a nose like a banana and inch-thick glasses, but the mothers will find you handsome indeed and encourage you to call them Mom and join the family for frequent Sunday dinners. Not being fools, they recognize a good match when they see one, by God.

Or say you're going to medical school or West Point or anyplace else that will make you appear more glamorous than you really are. Such people are regarded as winners by most of society, and people (girls) like to be associated with winners.

Of course, if you've majored in four years of wood shop it'll be a little harder to pull medical school off, but what have you got to lose? Most people tend to believe what you tell them; it saves wear and tear on their gray matter if they don't think any more often than absolutely necessary.

Again, be creative. Come up with your own scheme. Remember, it's all based on sleight-of-hand and bullshit. Anything that makes you appear to be something better than the real you is worth exploring. Such thinking will not only get you a first-rate date for the school prom, it'll also bring you fame and riches ever after.

Now for the prom itself. Go first-class. Rent a limo and get a tux and take a room in a good hotel for the after-prom party. Spare no expense in making it a truly memorable night. Your date will be ever so grateful; so grateful, in fact, that it may be a good idea for you to scarf a plate of oysters in preparation for the big event.

And don't forget that we live in the 21$^{st}$ century, an enlightened era which has put women on a full par with men and made us equal in every way—so you could make her pay for her share of the expenses. Give her a pass on this one, though, and foot the bill yourself. After all, it's her prom too and you don't want to ruin it for her by bringing in the NOW people.

In summary, enjoy your prom. Have a good time. Play the high roller for one night even if it's the last time you ever do so. Start early and don't go home before dawn. Dance the night away even as your years of innocence fade into the approaching cruel light of day and the real world closes in on you and yours.

You're a bona-fide high school graduate now and the world awaits without.

## Chapter Thirty-Seven

### After Graduation What?

Okay, so you buy this book as a freshman and, by studying it carefully and following its rules to the letter, you manage to survive high school and even graduate from same and the principal hands you a diploma and you go out and party and the next day you wake up and then what happens?

Are all your troubles over? Are you kidding? They've only just begun!

Consider. For most of you there's more school waiting and that means you're going right back to the equivalent of high school again. More books and half-crazy teachers and homework and dreariness. Or you might go into the armed forces and you have no idea what real dreariness is until the Marines ship your ass over to some place like Iraq and let you languish there for a couple of years in imminent danger of grave bodily harm.

Eventually, though, you'll finish school or the army and then you'll have to go to work. One or two of you will land some glamorous job like directing movies or exploring lost continents or performing open heart surgery, but the rest of you will end up chained to a desk in an office or putting in eighteen-hour days running your own donut shop. You'll look back fondly on your high school years as a time of delicious irresponsibility and carefree living that you may never experience again.

And you'll get married. If you're smart this will not happen before you're really old enough for it, say about thirty or thirty-five or so. Most of you won't marry the cheerleaders since there are hardly enough of them to go around for the star footballers. You'll end up marrying the girl in your history class with the braces but that's okay since you'll be twenty-five pounds overweight yourself and reek of cheap cigars. In other words, you'll probably get what you deserve.

In due time you'll have children, but not more than one or two if you know what's good for you. As wonderful as they can be, kids have a tendency to affect your life in wildly unanticipated ways, but nature prevents most people from seeing it coming in order to assure the continuation of the species.

Before you know it your kids will grow up and you'll be a fifty-year-old-dude with a paunch and wonder what the hell happened to you—and if you could possibly have avoided it. It is, after all, the way of the world.

During all this you'll look back at high school as a magical place where you dreamed dreams of a bright future and so it is if you play your cards right.

# Epilogue

Grandpa Ganja's keen mind is always at work, thinking ahead, planning the next caper, and that's what I've done here. You see, I have something I wanted to tell you, something very important, but I knew you wouldn't listen to me if I couldn't get your attention. So I laid a clever trap.

I figured if I could write a book that you guys really wanted to read, maybe one that was funny, or about true things, or even just brilliantly written you might listen to me. If you've read this far you must have found it funny, true or brilliant (or all three), and that means you're at the last chapter where I wanted you. So don't stop reading now or you'll miss out on the best part.

It's about dropping out of school. Did you know that 30% of American kids do not finish high school? That's not a new number; the dropout rate is always 30%, but this isn't the 1940s when we had jobs for everybody and diplomas weren't as important then to get work. That's not true today. Any job worth having requires at least a high school diploma these days so you have no real choice if you want a decent life down the road.

And now Grandpa Ganja has a confession to make. The fact is that I am a high school dropout. That's right, I didn't like school or the teachers and I thought I knew more than they did, so I quit in the eleventh grade and joined the Marines in '48. It took me about a week to find out I'd made a bad mistake, one that almost proved fatal when I ended up in Korea just in time to run into 500,000 Chinese guys who wanted to kill me.

I foiled them, though, by being elusive and quick on my feet and managed to escape without a scratch, but I still get jumpy when I see 500,000 Chinese guys in one place and they're all looking at me.

I left the Marines in '52 (they were glad to see me go) and headed straight back to school to fix my mistake. I got my high school diploma, enrolled in college, earned three degrees, and became a teacher in Detroit where I taught school for thirty years. If dropping out was dumb, going back to school was the smartest thing I ever did.

So that's what this chapter is all about. It's about staying in school and getting diplomas and doing smart things instead of dumb ones. It's about learning from my mistake and you not making the same one yourself. I had to waste four years to find out how important education is, but you don't have to do that because you're smarter than I was then and know Grandpa Ganja would never give you a bum steer.

It's about more than just getting a diploma, too. Education does things to people, it changes them inside, makes them feel better about themselves, more confident and comfortable with other people. As you learn more about things you learn more about yourself, and the more you know about who you are the better decisions you'll make in life.

But modern high schools offer more than just insight; they offer all kinds of practical stuff that will help you pay the rent later. Besides the usual college prep curriculum, they have business courses (typing, bookkeeping, business law, retailing); shop courses (auto mechanics, welding, electronics, woodworking, machine shop); magnet schools (health care careers, nurses aides, lab technicians) all designed to help you get a good job someday.

A few courses in bookkeeping will get you a well-paying job when you graduate. An accounting course in a community college can even make you an accountant and you can rig the books for some future corporate crooks. Good typists can always find work. Mechanics make good money and most of them start with high school courses, and trade schools are always looking for high school grads for their apprentice programs.

In other words, taking the right courses in high school can give you good skills for a lifetime job if you're smart enough to see that now and not ten years after you drop out. Talk to your teachers. Believe it or not, they want you to succeed. Teachers are pleased as punch when their students do well and will do whatever they can to help you. Let them know you care and want to do good work. Ask them for help or advice or even a small loan and they'll be delighted to work with you.

Take part in your classes. Make up a good

question and write it down and ask it in class. Teachers love that stuff and they'll mark you down as a winner. Always have your work done on time and done right, even if you have to skip your favorite TV show. Show up every day. Sit up straight, look alert, listen to what's being said so you can learn something and not waste your time.

If possible, take part in school activities. Join the school band, try out for the football squad or be a cheerleader, sign up for the drama club or the debating team. Most of the kids doing this stuff are a cut above the rest and these are the guys you want to hang out with.

Your loutish pals that hang out in the johns will be career louts and that job doesn't pay well, as there is always an abundance of louts that drives their wages down.

The trick is to look around and see what's going on and try to understand where you're heading. What do you want? Will you get it if you continue to do what you're doing now?

Is there a special job you'd like? Teacher? F.B.I. agent? Fireman? Doctor/nurse? Lawyer? Scientist? Computer expert? Soldier? Engineer? Used-car salesman? Truck driver? Corporate crook? Famous chef? Business owner?

What are the requirements for these jobs? Are there courses you should take now to be a future F.B.I. agent? Will you need special math skills? Or have to know how to shoot a gun? Or be able to speak Spanish?

Or know karate?

The time to find out is now. Tell your counselor what your plans are and ask for help. You want to learn as much about that career as you can and your counselor can provide the information to help you prepare for it. It's not a good idea to plan on an engineering career while you take four years of easy math courses and can't handle fractions well.

Another thought. Learning doesn't stop when you get your diploma. Lots of people whose formal schooling ended very early have gone on to a first-rate education by reading and studying on their own. They've even got a name for a self-taught person: autodidact. Nothing says a teacher is required in order for you to learn. Everyone is in charge of his own personal education and how much and what quality of learning he gets is ultimately up to him.

Finally, then, don't be an ignoramus like Grandpa Ganja back in '48. Stay in school and work at it, actually try to put the time to good use and learn something for a change. Your whole life will be better for it, your teachers will be delighted, your parents will be flabbergasted, your friends will respect you, and you'll grow taller and wiser and handsomer/prettier and have a wonderful life.

In a word, instead of merely surviving high school make it the start of your own growth as an intelligent and informed human being and you'll be glad you did—and so will the rest of us.

The choice is yours; make sure it's the right one.

The End

www.ingramcontent.com/pod-product-compliance
Lightning Source LLC
Chambersburg PA
CBHW051756040426
42446CB00007B/398